LAS VEGAS
and
LAUGHLIN
NEVADA

WE'RE ALWAYS WITH YOU.℠

Automobile Club of Southern California

Cover photo:
   Paris–Las Vegas

ISBN: 1-56413-560-8

Printed in the United States of America

Table of Contents

Las Vegas & Laughlin, Nevada

Southern Nevada is a land of extremes and contrasts: mega-resorts and huge dams, bizarre rock formations and noisy gambling halls, bespangled showgirls and fuzzy burros, thrill rides and wedding chapels.... People love it and hate it, sometimes all at once. But from the barren desert to the most elaborate casinos and hotels, Southern Nevada and all its offerings cannot be ignored.

Las Vegas is one of the nation's favorite vacation destinations. It's a 24-hour city where gambling reigns supreme and dreams of striking it rich sometimes come true. But Las Vegas has many facets, and casino action is just one of them. It also offers luxurious resort lodgings, top-name entertainment, world-class golf courses, scenic desert treks, nearby water recreation, and in recent years, plenty of activities for children. Las Vegas is home to 18 of the 20 largest resort hotels in the U.S.—top of the list being the 5034-room MGM Grand Hotel & Casino. Not surprisingly, there are also more hotel rooms here than any other city in the world: 124,210, with more on the way. In the year 2000, Las Vegas attracted an estimated 35.8 million visitors, a figure that seems to just keep growing.

Laughlin, by contrast, offers a more relaxed atmosphere than its flashy northern counterpart. It is an oasis along the Colorado River, where the state lines of California, Nevada and Arizona merge. Like Las Vegas, Laughlin offers plenty of gaming action, but the river remains one of its strongest assets. The area, which includes neighboring **Bullhead City, Arizona**, has long been known as a

Theme hotels now dominate the Las Vegas Strip.

Laughlin has become a boomtown on the banks of the Colorado River.

haven for "snowbirds" in winter (travelers from cold climes who migrate during the winter to Sunbelt states) and the river crowd in summer. Boating, fishing, water-skiing and swimming in the river's surprisingly frigid waters are favorite pursuits of vacationers, especially during the sizzling heat of summer. Combine the lure of the river with reasonably priced rooms, countless buffets, and even an international airport, and it should be no surprise that Laughlin has gained such a foothold in the West. More than 4.6 million tourists visited this small desert community in 2000.

Another town quickly making a name for itself is **Primm**, located along I-15, 40 miles south of Las Vegas at the California-Nevada border. Once just a mere drive-through known as Stateline, the settlement now boasts one of the world's tallest and fastest roller coasters, and is the site of three large resort-style hotels, a 6500-seat arena, a monorail and various other attractions.

Climate

Las Vegas experiences about 320 days of sunshine per year and an average high temperature of 80 degrees Fahrenheit. This high-desert community has an arid climate, low humidity and a yearly rainfall of about 4 inches. Spring and fall generally bring the mildest weather, when daytime highs are in the comfortable 70-degree range. Winter months, by contrast, can be quite cool, with highs in the 50s and lows in the 30s.

At the peak of summer, the temperature often climbs above 100 degrees. But the heat is easily escaped via air conditioning, swimming pools or jaunts to water parks. Scenic Mount Charleston in the Spring Mountains National Recreation Area also offers a break from the heat with its cooler upper-elevation temperatures.

Laughlin is located on the northeast edge of the Mojave Desert and has a high mean temperature of about 85 degrees. In this hot, dry region, the

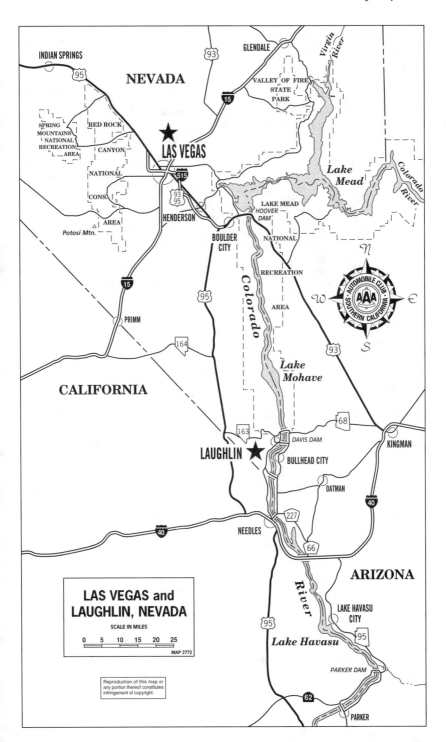

LAS VEGAS and
LAUGHLIN, NEVADA

SCALE IN MILES

0   5   10   15   20   25

MAP 2772

♠ Showing the Way

To guide travelers through the area's varied and sometimes staggering array of attractions, the Automobile Club of Southern California created this book as a reference to the many activities, points of interest and places to stay in Las Vegas, Laughlin and surrounding areas. In addition to *Las Vegas and Laughlin, Nevada*, the Auto Club produces a number of companion publications. The *Explore! Colorado River Guide Map* covers the area from Lake Mead to Yuma, and provides thorough map coverage and information on recreation and local attractions. Another publication covering nearby areas is the *San Bernardino County* map, which offers a recreation guide, listings for points of interest and detailed maps. These publications are available to AAA members at Auto Club district offices, as well as to nonmembers at selected California booksellers.

summer months routinely sizzle above the 100-degree mark, sometimes climbing above 120 degrees. But relief is always close at hand in the form of air conditioning and the frigid water of the Colorado River. Sometimes higher-than-average humidity triggers summer thunderstorms and flash floods, turning the area's dry washes into turbulent rivers. Winters can be equally severe with below-freezing temperatures. Rainfall averages about 4 inches a year.

Activities for Children

Because Las Vegas and Laughlin are usually considered adult-oriented cities, visitors in the past have often left children at home. Today, however, both desert communities offer many diversions for the younger set. Nearly all the larger hotels have some form of entertainment for children. Some even offer supervised children's programs, which allow adults the freedom to investigate the more mature attractions, while the children do whatever it is that children do. These facilities typically offer arts and crafts, video games, jungle gyms, puzzles and group play activities. Basketball, table

tennis, pool and even food service are available at some centers. Admission requirements vary from facility to facility; parents should call about reservations, restrictions and fees. Additional child-care services in Las Vegas and Laughlin may be found by referring to the telephone directory yellow pages under "Baby Sitters."

While day care is strictly for children, Las Vegas' many other youth-oriented attractions will entertain both the child and adult. The Stratosphere Tower, the tallest building west of the Mississippi, is crowned with two great thrill rides, including the highest roller coaster in the world. Year-round fun can be found at the Adventuredome, a five-acre, climate-controlled, indoor amusement park whose attractions include a water flume ride with a 60-foot free-fall, and the nation's only double-loop, double-corkscrew, indoor roller coaster. Circus Circus Hotel & Casino boasts a carnival-style arcade and circus acts.

Mandalay Bay's Shark Reef puts some teeth in the aquarium experience, with over 2000 animals from 100 different species, including manta rays, sea turtles and crocodiles. Exhibits are appropriate for all ages, with touch tanks geared to kids.

New York-New York Hotel & Casino's lures include the Manhattan Express roller coaster, and Coney Island Emporium, which offers an accumulation of midway-style carnival games. In addition to the blindingly bright beam shooting out from the apex of it's pyramid structure, the Luxor has an enormous sphinx out front and an eclectic mix of Egyptian replicas, including a full-size reproduction of King Tut's tomb.

Las Vegas has other attractions that also appeal to children. The Excalibur Hotel & Casino's medieval castle-themed exterior and Renaissance village interior are reminiscent of the legend of King Arthur. Strolling performers, carnival-style arcade games and nightly jousting tournaments can all be found here, as well as Merlin's Magic Motion Machine, a motion-simulator ride.

Treasure Island's spectacular pirate show features swashbucklers battling it out right in front of the hotel on Las Vegas Boulevard. Dazzling, fiery explosions and even the sinking of a ship provide exciting entertainment for all ages. A spectacular manmade volcano, located at the entrance to the Mirage, erupts nightly, spewing fire and smoke—and stopping traffic on Las Vegas Boulevard. Dramatic night lighting makes the adjacent five-story waterfall appear to be flowing lava. Inside the hotel, children will enjoy the Dolphin Habitat and Secret Garden as well as the white tiger display.

GameWorks, a huge virtual-reality arcade, has almost 300 video games of all description. It also features Surge Rock, at 75 feet one of the world's tallest freestanding, manmade rock-climbing structures. Other venues of

Kids can scale new heights at GameWorks'
Surge Rock attraction.

Rafting on the Colorado River is just one of many recreational activities available in the Las Vegas region.

interest to young people include the Imperial Palace Auto Collection, Las Vegas Natural History Museum, Las Vegas Mini Gran Prix, Lied Discovery Children's Museum, MGM Grand's Lion Habitat, Nevada State Museum and Historical Society, New York-New York's new ESPN Zone, Scandia Family Fun Center, Southern Nevada Zoological-Botanical Park and Wet 'n Wild. Details about these attractions can be found in the *Las Vegas Valley* chapter.

Destinations in and around Las Vegas that promote enjoyment of the outdoors include Oatman, Arizona, an Old West mining town. A group of friendly but wild burros roam Oatman's streets, often greeting visitors in hopes of a carrot snack. Entertaining gunfights are staged daily, and the town is fraught with small antique and souvenir shops that may be of interest to older children.

Natural attractions include Valley of Fire State Park and Red Rock Canyon National Conservation Area, which offer dramatic views of towering rust-colored sandstone formations and abundant opportunities for hiking and picnicking. A few miles from Red Rock Canyon, children will enjoy the petting zoo, miniature train rides and staged gunfights at Bonnie Springs Old Nevada. Only 45 minutes from Las Vegas is Spring Mountains National Recreation Area (part of Humboldt-Toiyabe National Forest), where mountain scenery, cooler temperatures and, in season, snow-skiing can be found.

Lake Mead National Recreation Area, 20 miles east of Las Vegas, has year-round fishing, swimming, hiking and picnicking, as well as guided tours of magnificent Hoover Dam. Children might also be interested to see American Indian petroglyphs in Grapevine Canyon or the local artifacts at the Colorado River Museum. (See listings in the *Laughlin-Bullhead City* chapter.)

Visitors to Primm will find the Desperado roller coaster and other thrill rides, while Henderson touts the Ethel M Chocolates Factory and Ron Lee's World of Clowns, all appealing to the young ones.

Laughlin's entertainment is geared mostly toward gaming, but parents will find plenty of activities to entertain their children in and around the gambling centers. The Colorado Belle, Edgewater, Flamingo Laughlin, Gold River, Harrah's Laughlin, Pioneer, Ramada Express and Riverside hotels all have video arcades. First-run movies are shown at Don Laughlin's Riverside Resort Hotel and at theaters in Bullhead City. Boat trips on the Colorado River offer both fresh air and adventure, and auto enthusiasts

should definitely make time to see the exotic cars at Don Laughlin's Classic Car Collection. The Ramada Express has a narrow-gauge railroad with a steam locomotive that takes passengers for a ride around the property.

Shopping

Most of the big resort hotels in Las Vegas and Laughlin have shopping venues. These usually feature a dozen or so stores selling designer fashions, furs, jewelry, artwork, toys and international gifts. Shopping at Mandalay Bay provides access to fine wines, original artwork, leather goods and jewelry. The opulent shops of Via Bellagio present creations from European

Friendly engineers and conductors take passengers around the parking lot on a narrow-gauge train at the Ramada Express Hotel in Laughlin.

♠ TIPPING

A tip or gratuity for services rendered is customary in Las Vegas, as it is in any U.S. city. Although entirely at the customer's discretion, prompt, friendly and good-quality service traditionally merits a tip. In Las Vegas and Laughlin, there is an especially staggering array of service personnel—all who supplement their income with tips—including card dealers, slot people, showroom maitre d's and pool attendants. When in doubt about the amount, 15 to 20 percent of the total bill is usually appropriate. Following are some helpful guidelines:

Bartenders/Cocktail Servers—For parties of two to four people, a tip of $1-2 per round is standard; more for larger groups.

Bell Captains, Bellhops, Skycaps—Luggage is usually tipped at $2-3 per bag or $5-10 if you have several bags. If you plan on using the concierge or VIP services for arrangements for shows, travel or car, a $5-10 tip is appropriate.

Child-care Attendants—Baby-sitting is no easy task, so a tip of $2-5 for two to four hours of child-care service is appreciated.

Dealers—It is customary make a small bet for the dealer or tip a chip when you are winning.

Hotel Maids—A tip upon departure of $2-5 per day is appreciated.

Lounge Attendants—Approximately $1-2 in the attendant's tray is appropriate for being handed towels, soap, etc.

Masseuse/Masseur—The 15- to 20-percent rule is standard.

Pool Attendants—Fifty cents to $1 is customary for towels, pads, lounges, etc.

Slot People/Keno Runners—A $1 tip now and then is appropriate for good service from keno runners and slot people.

Taxi Drivers—A 10- to 20-percent tip is expected for a direct route, more if the driver is friendly and helps with the door and your luggage.

Tour Guides—A tip of $1-2 per person at the end of the trip is suggested.

Valet Parking Attendants—A tip of $2 is standard.

Waiters/Room Service—The 15- to 20-percent rule applies for both. With room service, the tip is sometimes included in the bill; be sure to ask when you place your order.

Desert Passage at the Aladdin is one of the city's more exotic shopping malls.

designers and fine jewelers. A French shopping district at Paris Las Vegas includes a French wine shop and a pastry store. Aladdin, not to be outdone, offers Desert Passage, an open-air bazaar complete with street peddlers. (See the *Las Vegas Valley* chapter for more detailed listings.)

The larger hotels are also good places to find shops that carry such necessities as aspirin, toothbrushes, film, postage stamps, magazines and other miscellaneous items. These shops are usually centrally located near the front entrance of the hotel, the registration desk or the casino.

For the real souvenir hound there is also no shortage of trinket shops. Hats, shirts, coffee mugs, salt and pepper shakers, genuine leather purses, turquoise jewelry, dice, playing cards and poker chips are widely available. In Las Vegas, these shops are mainly along the Strip area of Las Vegas Boulevard from Charleston Boulevard south to Tropicana Avenue. Downtown, they are located one block off Fremont between Main and 4th streets.

History

Las Vegas is Spanish for "The Fertile Plain," so named for its numerous springs and once verdant landscape. The surrounding harsh and unforgiving Mojave Desert protected this oasis for centuries from all but the native Paiute Indians. It was not until 1829 when the first known inhabitants of European descent settled. By comparison, Laughlin is a much more recent arrival, beginning in 1966 with Don Laughlin's aerial view of this once barren, formidable landscape. From his private plane, the native Midwesterner saw investment potential along a vacant stretch of the Colorado River, near Davis Dam and the sparsely populated town of Bullhead City, Arizona.

The discovery of abundant spring water at what is now **Las Vegas** shortened the Spanish Trail to Los Angeles, eased the rigors for Spanish traders and hastened the rush west for California gold. Some 14 years later, John C. Frémont, an American soldier and explorer, led an overland expedition west and camped at Las Vegas Springs. Today, Fremont Street and numerous other area landmarks carry his name.

The modern history of Las Vegas began in 1855, when a small group of Mormon settlers arrived. They came to protect the mail route between Los Angeles and Salt Lake City, but for the next three years also cultivated fruits and vegetables and mined lead at Potosi Mountain.

The Mormons abandoned their mining activity when the bullets made from their ore proved to be flaky and brittle due to an extremely high silver content—a problem other miners would liked to have had. American Indian raiding parties also added to their problems. The Mormons' 150-square-foot adobe fort was abandoned in 1858; a portion of it can be seen today near the intersection of Las Vegas Boulevard North and Washington Avenue (see Old Las Vegas Mormon Fort State Historic Park in the *Las Vegas Valley* chapter).

In 1864 Nevada was admitted to the Union as the 36th state, although the 11,000 square miles surrounding Las Vegas were part of the Arizona territory. It was not until two years later that Congress ceded this region to Nevada, establishing the current state borders.

Farming and ranching were the main economic focus of Las Vegas until the coming of the railroad. On May 15, 1905, the Union Pacific Railroad auctioned off 1200 lots in a single day—lots that soon sprouted gambling houses, saloons and stores. In 1910 Nevada passed an anti-gambling law so strict that it even forbade the Western custom of flipping a coin for the price of a drink. Despite the law, which remained in effect for 20 years, gambling continued to flourish in the form of "underground" games, where patrons uttered a secret password to play.

Legalized gambling returned to the state in 1931, at the height of the Great Depression. It was also the same year construction started on the Boulder Canyon Project. Thousands of jobless citizens, victims of the nation's economic slump, streamed into the Las Vegas-Boulder City area for work. At its peak, the project employed 5128 people and had an average monthly payroll of $500,000.

Fremont Street (1929) as Las Vegas awaits inspection as a housing center for thousands of Boulder Dam (Hoover Dam) construction workers.

In 1935 President Franklin Roosevelt dedicated the structure, known then as Boulder Dam. In April 1947, by congressional action, the 726-foot-high structure was officially designated Hoover Dam, the name by which it is known today.

The great hydroelectric project on the Colorado River originally brought power to Las Vegas, and this abundant source of electricity helped create the famous neon city. (Today Las Vegas' power primarily comes from coal-burning power stations.) In 1941 a group of Los Angeles investors, speculating on the resort potential of the area, built El Rancho Vegas, the first hotel on what became the Las Vegas Strip. Shortly thereafter, the Last Frontier was completed, followed by the fabulous Flamingo, a hotel and casino built by the infamous mobster Benjamin "Bugsy" Siegel. (Six months after the Flamingo's December 1946 opening, Siegel was murdered by an unknown assailant in Beverly Hills, California.)

The momentum established by these early resorts has continued ever since, taking off in the post-World War II years as the town emerged to become a major tourist destination. High-rise hotels with blazing marquees began to rise along a stretch of Las Vegas Boulevard that would soon be known as simply the Strip. The Desert Inn, Sands, Riviera, Dunes and Stardust were but a few of those to open during the 1950s, and their names soon became familiar far beyond the Nevada state line.

Casino gambling was the main draw at most venues, but entertainment helped seal Las Vegas' reputation as a playground getaway. In 1941, when El Rancho Vegas was the only Strip resort, singers, comedians, strippers and other performers entertained guests in its small, intimate showroom.

Other resorts copied that successful format by featuring big-name entertainers of their own. Comedian Jimmy Durante and pianist Liberace were among the first headliners to play Las

Vegas. The Stardust blazed a new path in the 1950s when it made a stage-spectacular its main entertainment feature. The hotel imported *Lido de Paris* from France, a critically acclaimed show that enjoyed a 31-year run. The Tropicana followed suit with another French import when it bought the U.S. rights to the *Folies Bergere* in 1960. It remains a favorite to this day, complete with its trademark show-stopping cancan number.

Casino lounges emerged during the post-war years, offering dusk-to-dawn entertainment while spawning such crowd-pleasers as Don Rickles and Bob Newhart. For insurance, the hotels began importing the likes of Judy Garland and Red Skelton from Hollywood on a regular basis. Meanwhile, the famed "Rat Pack" of Frank Sinatra, Dean Martin and Sammy Davis Jr. crooned to hundreds of sellout audiences during their hey-days in the 1950s and '60s. Sinatra would remain a star attraction decades later, packing the crowds into the early 1990s.

While headliners like Debbie Reynolds, Wayne Newton and Siegfried & Roy have become synonymous with Las Vegas in recent decades, no one did more for the town's entertainment image than the "King" himself, Elvis Presley. By 1964, when he romanced Ann-Margaret in the movie *Viva Las Vegas*, he had established himself as a major Strip attraction, and his greatest glory days still lay ahead. Between 1969 and 1976, Presley performed to more than 1500 sellout crowds at the Las Vegas Hilton, a one-man windfall for the town's tourism business.

Though gambling remained the number one lure, in 1976 the town faced competition for the first time when New Jersey voters approved a ballot measure to open casinos in Atlantic City. Las Vegas confronted the challenge by transforming itself to a family-friendly destination. As early as 1968, Circus Circus opened on the Strip, with carnival games and midway-style rides beneath its circus tent-shaped roof, but the transformation did not take off until the late 1980s.

When the Mirage opened in 1989, it featured a white tiger habitat, dolphin pool and man-made volcano among its many non-casino attractions. A year later came the Excalibur, a 4000-room property designed like a medieval castle, with jousting knights, court jesters and entire floors devoted to non-gambling entertainment. The '90s building frenzy was under way, reaching its peak in late 1993 when three huge properties, the Luxor, Treasure Island and MGM Grand, opened within three months of each other. With over 5000 rooms, the $1 billion MGM Grand became the world's largest hotel property.

While the 1993, 12,000-room, single-year growth has not been eclipsed, growth continues, and with it a trend toward opulence. The 1998 opening of the most expensive hotel property in history, the $1.7 billion Bellagio, demonstrated a continued faith in the ability of Las Vegas to attract high rollers. The elegant hotel features an indoor botanical garden and a restaurant with original works of art by Picasso. Mandalay Bay Resort and Casino, which opened in 1999, incorporates a tropical theme throughout its property, featuring an 11-acre wave pool, the Shark Reef aquarium, and a House of Blues.

In a town where bigger has always been better, a new breed of resort is establishing itself. Modeling and miniaturization are their focus. New

El Rancho Vegas was the first resort on The Strip when it opened in 1941.

York, Venice and Paris have been scaled and relocated in a way that could only be Vegas. The Statue of Liberty, the Empire State Building and the Chrysler Building re-create the Big Apple's skyline at New York-New York. Romantic Venice is found at the Venetian, complete with gondoliers plying canals, the Ca D'Oro (Palace of Gold), the Bridge of Sighs and even the Rialto Bridge. Paris Las Vegas features a 50-story replica of the Eiffel Tower, where 100 feet above the Strip guests may dine in a gourmet restaurant, or ride a glass elevator to the top to an observation deck that provides panoramas of the city.

Adding to the concept of the city as "a Disneyland for adults" is the construction of the ultramodern, $650-million Las Vegas Monorail. The privately-funded project, slated for completion early in 2004, will include six casino stops and enable visitors to travel from one end of the Strip to the other in 15 minutes.

Population has grown dramatically in recent years, as Las Vegas swelled from 258,000 residents in 1990 to over 484,000 by mid-2000. Likewise, Clark County is now home to more than 1.4 million people, compared to 768,000 a decade ago. By county planners' estimates that figure could top 1.9 million by the year 2010.

Perhaps befitting that growth, Las Vegas has never paid great homage to its history, choosing instead to focus on tomorrow. As an example, when the Hilton Corporation tore down an older section of the Flamingo Hotel in 1993, it also razed the fortress-like "Bugsy Suite" with its false stairways and bulletproof office that the famed gangster used before his death. The Flamingo name survives, but each year entire hotels of bygone eras are felled to clear the way for bigger, more elaborate resorts than ever before.

Even when Las Vegas does preserve the past, it reinvents itself in order to adapt to the ever-changing tastes of visitors. Take Fremont Street, the one-time "Glitter Gulch," which lost out years ago to the Strip as the center of gambling and entertainment action. A four-block section of the street was closed to traffic in 1995 and transformed into the Fremont Street Experience, a pedestrian mall crowned by a 90-foot-high canopy with more than 2 million lights. The street now hosts a series of dazzling sound and light shows on the hour every night.

As the 21st century unfolds, water shortfalls may slow the region's long-term growth. Most of Las Vegas' water comes from the Colorado River, which Nevada must share with seven other states. If present trends continue, the state will use up its allotment, which will curtail growth if new supplies are not developed.

Before 1966, what is now **Laughlin** was composed of one roadhouse restaurant at the end of a dirt road. The area was known as South Pointe, the name of a construction camp that housed workers for nearby Davis Dam. (South Pointe's population disappeared following completion of the dam in 1953.) Entrepreneur Don Laughlin, fresh from a successful 10-year gaming venture in Las Vegas, purchased and renovated the deteriorating restaurant as a casino in 1966, appropriately naming it Riverside. In 1977 the growing community was officially named after its entrepreneur-founder.

Initially, Laughlin's customers were residents of Bullhead City, enticed by the free ferry service from a parking lot on the Arizona side of the river. As news of the friendly, informal atmosphere of the Riverside Casino got out, people from greater distances showed up. Soon the new business was a great success, which induced Laughlin to expand his operation. Others quickly saw the potential for the gaming business along the shores of the Colorado, so beginning in 1967 with what is now the Golden Nugget (originally called the Bob Cat), additional casino/hotels began to rise. Today nine major casinos occupy the west riverbank of the Colorado at Laughlin; another sits a block back from the water, and still another lies nine miles to the south of town on the Fort Mojave Indian Reservation. Those casinos were the main draw to the 4.6 million people who visited Laughlin in 2000.

Laughlin supplanted Lake Tahoe in 1987 as Nevada's third-largest gaming resort (after Las Vegas and Reno), and plans for further growth are a major topic of local conversation. Laughlin has clearly come a long way from its humble beginnings, when coyotes outnumbered the town's population. The town's 8100 residents are still outnumbered, however, this time by more than 11,000 slot machines.

Across the river in **Bullhead City,** the boomtown atmosphere is equally intense. Rugged mountains provide a scenic backdrop and contain mines and ghost towns of historic importance. Katherine Mine, Chloride and Oatman give travelers an enticing glimpse into the world of the Wild West. More than 29,000 people reside in Bullhead City today.

With wonderfully jagged mountaintops, winding roads and alluring vistas, a drive along Historic Route 66 through **Oatman** and **Kingman**, Arizona, is pleasing to the eye. It also serves as a reminder of those who, during the 1930s, migrated from the parched Midwest on this very road, seeking a better life.

Then there's **Primm,** the latest town to make a pitch for the hearts and wallets of visitors to Southern Nevada. Known for years as State Line, the town changed its name in 1996 to honor Gary Primm, who owned the three hotel-casinos in this outpost at the California border. Once just a dusty rest stop along I-15, Primm has become a destination in its own right with its modern hotel-casinos, thrill rides and golf course.

Casino Games

From 1931 until the mid-1970s, Nevada was the only state that offered legalized gambling. This fact alone helped make Las Vegas the single most popular tourist destination in the United States.

Before embarking on one of the many games of chance, it's a good idea to become familiar with a game's rules and strategy. Gambling instruction is offered in most casinos and, in some cases, on the hotel's cable television channel. Understanding a game's intricacies will not only increase your odds of winning but also make it more enjoyable to play. Do not expect dealers or croupiers to be of much help; they have a job to do and will offer assistance and advice only when they can. A good way to get to know a game is to watch the action for awhile before joining in; observation is a cheap way of learning some of the more obvious lessons.

Video poker is a favorite of casino patrons.

Many books devoted to the art of casino gambling have complete explanations of the rules, strategy, odds, wagering and systems that claim to give players an advantage. But be skeptical of the systems: statistically they might work in the long run, but few players have the time and the resources to last, or the concentration and mental dexterity that are often required. The serious student will spend time practicing at home before venturing into a casino. And a last piece of advice: Before placing any bets, determine how much you can afford to lose and set that money aside for gambling. Should it cross to the other side of the tables, don't dig for more! It is not just a cliché that people can lose everything they have.

BACCARAT A game very similar to chemin de fer, baccarat (pronounced Ba-Ca-Rah) is played with eight decks of cards dealt from a box called a "shoe." Two cards are given to each of two players, with one player being designated the bank. The object of the game is to come as close to the number nine as possible. All tens and face cards are counted as zero. Other people at the table bet on either the bank or the player.

BINGO Most bingo games in Las Vegas and Laughlin are played on "boards" with three bingo cards on each board. There is both open-play and party bingo at most casinos. In open-play bingo, each board costs between 10¢ and 40¢ per game. Party bingo is played at set hours; cards cost $1 to $4 each with a $3 to $6 minimum; approximately 10 to 12 games are played during each party session.

BLACKJACK Also called "21," blackjack is one of the most popular card games, mainly because it's fast and easy to learn. The object of the game is to beat the dealer by getting as close to 21 as possible without going over that count.

CARIBBEAN STUD POKER This game, based on Five Card Stud but played on a layout similar to Blackjack, is the first casino table game to offer a separate progressive jackpot in addition to regular wagers.

CRAPS The most complicated casino game, craps offers dozens of different ways to bet on the dice. The action is fast and the amount of money exchanging hands is considerable. Craps is not a good game for the timid, but it's fun to watch.

KENO This is an adaptation of an ancient Chinese game. Players mark a series of favorite numbers between one and 80 that appear on the blank keno ticket. Twenty numbers are then drawn at random. The amount of money won depends on the type of ticket played and how many winning numbers were selected. Many restaurants and lounges have keno runners who take the bets. Keno is also a popular slot game.

PAI GOW This ancient Chinese game involves 32 dominoes that are shuffled by the dealer and then placed in eight stacks of four each. Up to eight players are dealt one stack each. The object of the game is to set the four dominoes into two pairs for the best ranking combinations.

PAI GOW POKER A combination of poker and Pai Gow, this game is played with an ordinary deck of 52 cards plus one joker. The joker is used as an ace or to complete a straight or flush. Players are dealt seven cards each, which are arranged into two hands. One hand contains five cards and is known as the "high hand," while the other hand has only two cards and is called the "low hand." The object of the game is to win the bet by having both the high and low hands rank higher than the respective hands of the banker. The ranking is determined by traditional poker rules.

POKER The rules for casino poker are similar to home games, except that the house provides a dealer who manages the game without playing a hand. The house makes money by taking a small percentage of each pot. Five Card Stud is the best-known form of poker; the object of the game is to create the highest hand possible by taking or discarding the various cards dealt. Let It Ride is one of many variations. Check the rules carefully before sitting down at a game.

RACE AND SPORTS BOOKS Bets can be made on practically any horse race, boxing match, or professional or collegiate game (most Nevada events, except boxing matches, are excluded) from the comfort of race and sports books. Live events are shown on giant, satellite-fed screens. Most of the major hotels have race and sports books.

ROULETTE The roulette wheel has 36 numbers plus a green zero and a green double zero. Bets can be made on one number, a group, a color or a column of numbers. Odds on roulette range from 35-to-1 to even money. For example, if the player wins by betting on a single number, he or she is paid $35 for every $1 wagered. This is strictly a game of luck and intuition, so there's no reason to worry about skill level. Low stakes games are common, so a few dollars can keep a player going for quite some time.

SLOT MACHINES One-armed bandits and video poker comprise the majority of slots, but video blackjack, video keno and a variety of other games are offered. Quarter and dollar machines are the most prevalent, and most slots don't even require coins or tokens—they accept U.S. bills of many denominations. There are a variety of ways to win, including multiple pay lines, fixed jackpots and progressives (slots linked to statewide networks). To win the big jackpots and progressives requires more than the minimum bet; some machines accept up to 10 bets (or coins) at once.

Marriage Information

Two words spoken as often in Las Vegas as "hit me" and "double down" are without a doubt, "I do." Where else but in this unique community are marriage licenses issued so frequently (one every 5½ minutes), and where else would Elvis impersonators preside over the ceremonies? Seven days a week, 24 hours a day on weekends (correct change required), wedding vows are taken at drive-up windows, on bungee jumping platforms and boats, in helicopters, hotel suites and churches, and at dozens of wedding chapels. Ninety miles to the south, Laughlin now has its own branch of the Clark County Clerk's Office, and couples there can get hitched on the Colorado River aboard Mississippi-style riverboats or in any number of wedding chapels.

Marriages in **Las Vegas** total more than 100,000 per year, due in part to the ease of getting a marriage license. Historically, the most popular wedding day here is Valentine's Day, with New Year's Eve running a close second. Among the famous who have married in Las Vegas are Paul Newman and Joanne Woodward, Elvis and Priscilla Presley, Frank Sinatra and Mia Farrow, Richard Gere and Cindy Crawford, and Bruce Willis and Demi Moore.

A wedding and gondola ride at the Venetian.

To purchase a marriage license, the bride and groom must simply appear at the Marriage Bureau Office, located in the county courthouse at 200 South 3rd Street, or the Justice Court in Laughlin. No legal residency is required. Blood tests are not needed and there is no waiting period. Persons cannot be nearer of kin than second cousins or cousins of half blood. Persons ages 16 and 17 must have the consent of their parents or legal guardians. Persons giving consent must have proof of identity and guardianship; proof of age may be required as well. If the bride or groom was previously married, divorce must be final in the state in which it was granted; no papers are required. The office is open daily, Monday through Thursday from 8 a.m. to midnight, and continuously (24 hours) from 8 a.m. Friday to midnight Sunday; 24 hours on holidays. The license fee is $35 in cash. For information, call the Marriage Bureau Office at (702) 455-3156 or 455-4415.

Marriage ceremonies can be performed by the Commissioner of Civil Marriages, 309 South 3rd Street, or in one of the many wedding chapels in town (more than 50 at last count). The commissioner's office charges $35, and the hours are the same as the Marriage Bureau's. Wedding chapel fees depend on the elaborateness of the ceremony. One witness to the ceremony is required by law. Many of the large hotel or casino complexes have wedding chapels on the grounds. For a list of wedding chapels, see the Las Vegas telephone directory yellow pages under "Wedding."

An additional branch of the Marriage Bureau serves the community of **Laughlin.** Couples wishing to marry in this river city can obtain a license at the Justice Court Office in the Regional Government Center, 101 Civic Way. Licenses are issued Tuesday through Thursday from 8 a.m. to 4:30 p.m., Friday from 8 a.m. to 6 p.m. and Saturday from 10 a.m. to 4 p.m.; closed Sunday and Monday. No waiting period or blood test is required. All that is necessary is the $35 license fee in cash and proof of age. The Laughlin-Bullhead City area offers wedding services at several wedding chapels and aboard riverboats. Ceremonies can also be performed in the Justice Court Office (appointments are required). There is an additional $35 recording fee here for a total charge of $70. For more information, call the Justice Court Office at (702) 298-4622. Wedding chapels can be found in the Laughlin-Bullhead City telephone directory yellow pages under "Wedding Chapels and Ceremonies."

Las Vegas Valley

*Today's gambling meccas offer an array of activities for the whole family. Once geared to adults only, **Las Vegas** is now irresistibly child-friendly with roller coasters, water parks, virtual reality theaters, laser shows and museums.*

The biggest change, though, came with the 1990s' proliferation of huge, themed hotels. It's no longer enough to boast how many guest rooms you have or how "loose" the casino slots may be. Just drive the Strip, where traffic slows to a crawl while drivers shamelessly gawk at the huge pyramid and sphinx of the Egyptian-themed Luxor; the surreal white castle of the Excalibur, which salutes the legend of King Arthur; the soaring Manhattan skyline of New York-New York; or the snarling pirates and gallant sailors waging battle nightly in front of Treasure Island.

With hotels often filled to capacity, the continued growth seems to be unlimited. Without a doubt, audacious creativity, unabashed flamboyance and a dash of irreverence have proved a winning formula in wooing visitors to modern-day Las Vegas.

POINTS OF INTEREST

Attractions are listed alphabetically by city or area—**Henderson, Las Vegas** and **North Las Vegas**. Listings connected to hotel properties do not imply AAA endorsement for the lodging establishment.

Henderson

See **A Quick Guide to Las Vegas and Vicinity** in this chapter under Las Vegas.

BIRD VIEWING PRESERVE *2400 Moser Dr. (702) 566-2939. Open daily 6 am-3 pm. Free; guided tours by appointment.* This preserve, adjacent to a water reclamation facility, includes a visitor center, numerous trails and observation stations with benches.

Rolling stock at the Clark County Museum.

CLARK COUNTY MUSEUM *13 miles SE of Las Vegas at 1830 S Boulder Hwy (US 93/95). (702) 455-7955. Open daily 9 am-4:30 pm. Closed Jan 1 and Dec 25. Adults, $1.50; ages 55 and over and 3-15, $1.* This 25-acre museum houses regional memorabilia, historic structures and artifacts. Heritage Street's collection of six historic homes and commercial buildings includes many which have been fully restored to reflect the lifestyles of their respective eras. Other outdoor exhibits include authentic rolling stock, mining equipment and a "ghost town" comprised of several structures dating to the 1880s. The 8000-square-foot indoor Exhibit Center features specially themed displays, and a permanent Southern Nevada timeline exhibit that dates from prehistoric times to the present.

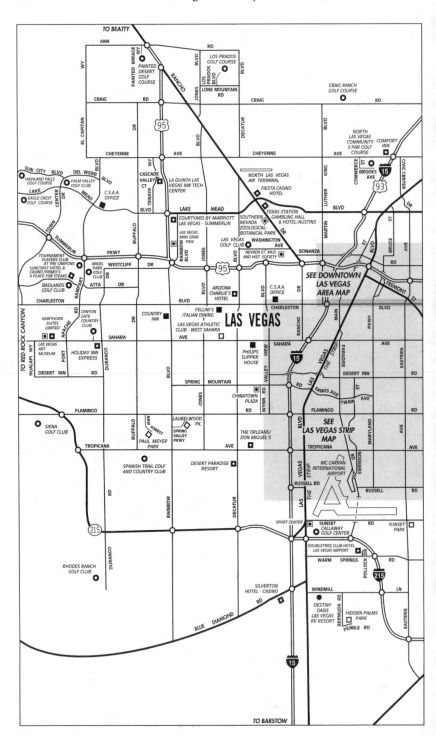

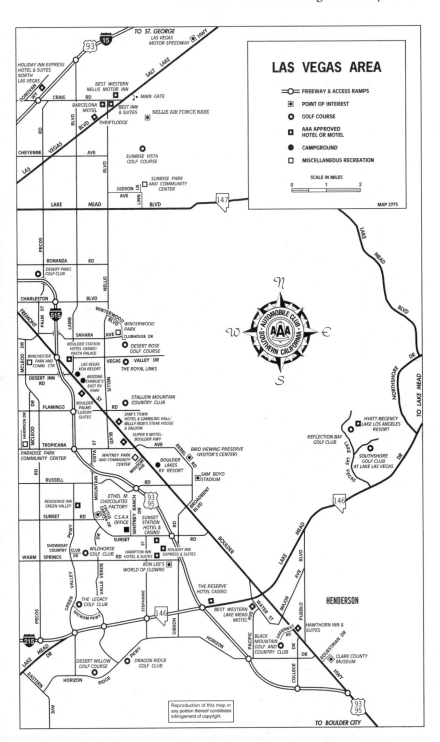

ETHEL M CHOCOLATES FACTORY
8 miles SE of the Strip, off Sunset Wy at Mountain Vista; 2 Cactus Garden Dr. Recorded information (702) 433-2500. Open daily 8:30 am-7 pm. Closed Thanksgiving and Dec 25. Free. Ethel M's self-guided tour offers a behind-the-scenes look at the ingredients and machinery used in the candy-making process. Adjacent to the factory is a 2½-acre cactus garden featuring rare and exotic plants. At the end of the tour, participants may sample their favorite Ethel M chocolate and shop for other tempting treats in the gift store.

RON LEE'S WORLD OF CLOWNS
Off Gibson and Warm Springs rds, at 330 Carousel Pkwy. (702) 434-1700. Open Mon-Fri 8:30 am-4:30 pm, Sat 10 am-4:30 pm. Closed Sun and major holidays. Free tour; carousel rides, $1. The mold-making and painting processes of clown figurines are shown during this self-guided tour. Through windows, visitors may watch the artisans at work; a video at each station explains the process being done. A large gift shop retails the final products. The facility also houses a gourmet cafe and a 30-foot Chance Carousel—a favorite with children.

Las Vegas

ADVENTUREDOME—*See Circus Circus Hotel & Casino.*

A.J. HACKETT BUNGY *810 Circus Circus Dr, adjacent to Circus Circus Hotel & Casino. (702) 385-4321. Open daily at 11 am; Mon-Fri to 8:30 pm, Sat-Sun to 10 pm; bungee jumpers must have registered to* jump at least ½ hour before closing time. $54 per person; same-day additional jumps, $20 per person. This New Zealand-based company has several locations around the world and a record of more than 1 million incident-free jumps. Participants plunge 171 feet from North America's highest double platform over a 12-foot pool. Video and T-shirt packages available.

ALADDIN RESORT & CASINO
3667 Las Vegas Blvd S, across from Bellagio. (702) 736-7114. The new luxury resort employs an exotic theme based on the legendary *1,001 Arabian Nights.* The casino, a 17-story Moroccan fantasy of cliffs and archways, houses the town's first European-style gaming club.

Blue Note Jazz Club *(702) 862-8307. Live jazz nightly at 8 and 10:30 pm; jam session Wed 9 pm. Restaurant open daily at 5 pm; Mon-Thu to 11 pm, Fri-Sun to midnight. Reservations recommended.* Like its New York counterpart, this club showcases blues and jazz musicians in a small club setting. There is also a full-service restaurant.

Desert Passage *(702) 866-0710. Open daily 10 am-midnight.* This 500,000-square-foot shopping mall is designed to look and feel like an open-air bazaar. Inspired by traditional trading areas in Bombay, Tangiers and Marrakesh, this shopping environment includes a 10-story terraced mountain and a North African harbor complete with indoor thunderstorms. In addition to 130 retail shops and 14 restaurants, roaming vendors hawk everything from meat-on-a-stick to jewelry to trinkets.

Bellagio's indoor Conservatory and Botanical Garden is an inviting spot.

BELLAGIO *3600 Las Vegas Blvd S, across from Paris Las Vegas. (702) 693-7111, (888) 987-6667. Shops open daily 10 am-midnight.* Named for a town on Italy's Lake Como, this resort is known for its elegant and distinctive Old World look. The grand front lobby has an 18-foot ceiling and museum-quality glass chandelier; the Conservatory and Botanical Garden features seasonal trees and flowers with theatrical lighting. Via Bellagio, a glass-enclosed shopping arcade, offers 100,000 square feet of upscale boutiques such as Giorgio Armani, Gucci, Chanel and Tiffany & Co.

Bellagio Gallery of Fine Art *Open daily 8 am-11 pm. $12 admission; reservations 7 days in advance for local guests, 90 days for out-of-town guests. Wheelchair accessible.* This gallery features rotating exhibits from major museums and private collections throughout the world, favoring the Impressionist Movement of the 1870s as well as contemporary artists. The hotel's Picasso restaurant displays original paintings and ceramic pieces by the famed artist.

Fountains of Bellagio *Shows daily every 15 minutes 7 pm-midnight, and every half-hour Mon-Fri 3-7 pm, Sat-Sun from noon. Free.* A fountain show takes place on the 8½-acre lake entrance to Bellagio, choreographed to music ranging from Pavarotti to Sinatra. Shows are announced with the chiming of bells in the nearby campanile.

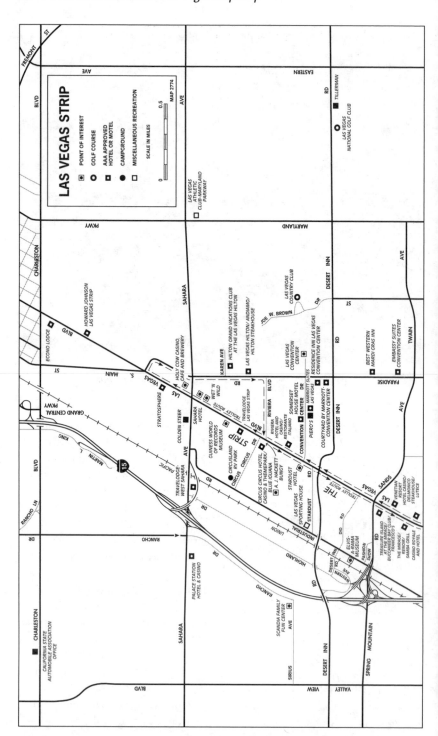

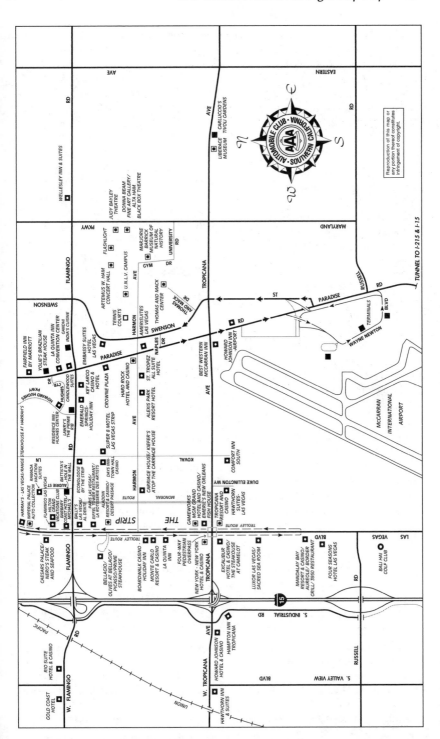

BUCCANEER BAY—*See Treasure Island.*

CAESARS PALACE *3750 Las Vegas Blvd S. (702) 731-7333.* The glory that was Rome is revived at this resort, where even the gift shop teddy bears wear togas. Amidst the "classical" architecture is the 50,000-gallon Atlantis Aquarium, featuring over 500 exotic tropical fish.

Caesars Magical Empire *Shows Tue-Sat 4:30-10 pm. $75. Tours Tue-Sat 11:30 am-3:30 pm. Free.* Magic, mystery and dining converge in this attraction, where visitors are entertained before and during their meals. Greeters dressed as Roman centurions lead guests to one of 10 dining chambers or two séance rooms, where a magician takes charge and performs an array of mystical feats during dinner. Tours of the dining and entertainment complex, including a *Lumineria* show with dancing, fire, smoke and lighting effects, are available during pre-dining hours.

Forum Shops *(702) 733-9000, (888) 910-7223. Open daily at 10 am; Sun-Thu to 11 pm, Fri-Sat to midnight.* This upscale indoor mall features a Roman motif, talking statues and a domed "sky" that changes from night to day. A 1997 expansion doubled the mall's size to 533,000 square feet, and established more than 110 shops and restaurants. *Atlantis*, the centerpiece for the expansion, is a hall 160 feet in diameter with an 85-foot-high ceiling that features animated figures.

The Race for Atlantis *(702) 733-9000, (888) 910-7223. Open daily at 10 am; Sun-Thu to 11 pm, Fri-Sat to midnight. Adults, $9.50; ages 55 and over, $8.50; ages 12 and under, $6.75 (42" height requirement).* The Race for Atlantis is the world's only 3-D IMAX motion simulator. Super-sized three-dimensional images and sound systems immerse guests in the experience through the use of a headset with a visor and personal sound system.

CHINATOWN PLAZA *W of the Strip; 4255 Spring Mountain Rd. (702) 221-8448, 222-0590. Open daily; store hours vary.* This shopping plaza has more than two dozen specialty shops that carry jewelry, handcrafted furniture, clothing and other merchandise from the Orient. In addition to several restaurants, one of the largest Asian supermarkets in Nevada is located here.

CIRCUS CIRCUS HOTEL, CASINO & THEMEPARK *2880 Las Vegas Blvd S. (702) 734-0410.* This resort, one of the town's original casino-theme parks, offers what is perhaps the quintessential Las Vegas experience.

Adventuredome *Recorded information (702) 794-3939. Open daily 10 am; closing times vary with season. Free admission; all-day ride pass, $18.95 for 48" and taller; $12.95 for 33-47"; individual ride ticket prices vary. Military and Nev. residents, $2 off adult pass.* The Adventuredome is a climate-controlled amusement park spanning five acres. Featured rides include the nation's only indoor double-loop, double-corkscrew roller coaster; a water flume ride with a 60-foot free fall; Hot Shots Laser Tag, a high-tech version of the old game of tag; Chaos, a new thrill ride; and a number of tamer attractions suitable for younger children. Themed gift shops, a restaurant and snack bar are also on premises.

Midway *Under the big top. Open daily 11 am-midnight. Performances every ½ hour. Free.* Circus acts include acrobatic antics on both the high and low wires, juggling, trapeze artists, animal acts and unicycle-balancing acts.

♠ *A Quick Guide to Las Vegas and Vicinity*

Population

City of Las Vegas 484,454

Clark County 1,428,690

Elevation 2174 ft.

Emergency 911

Police (nonemergency)

Boulder City (702) 293-9224

Henderson (702) 565-8933

Metropolitan Las Vegas,
Mount Charleston and
North Las Vegas (702) 649-9111

Highway Conditions
(702) 486-3116

Time (775) 844-1212

Weather

Las Vegas (702) 248-4800

Mount Charleston, Lake Mead
(702) 736-3854

**Emergency Road Service for
AAA Members**

(800) AAA-HELP
(in the USA and Canada)

(800) 464-0889
(for the hearing impaired)

Newspapers

The major daily newspapers are the
Las Vegas Review-Journal and the *Las
Vegas Sun*. The weekly publication
Today in Las Vegas and the biweekly
What's On, distributed in lodgings
and other tourist venues, provides
information on attractions, dining
and entertainment.

Radio Stations

These stations broadcast news,
weather and traffic. For a complete
list of radio programs, consult the
daily newspapers.

Highway News: KHWY (98.5 FM);
News/Sports/Talk: KBAD (920),
KDWN (720 AM), KENO (1460
AM), KLAV (1230 AM), KVBC
(105.1 FM), KNXT (840 AM),
KNEWS (970 AM); **Public
Radio/Classical**: KNPR (89.5 FM);
Spanish: KDOL (1280 AM).

TV Stations

The area's major television stations
include channels 3 (NBC), 5 (FOX),
8 (CBS), 10 (PBS), 13 (ABC), 21
(UPN), 33 (WB) and 39 (Spanish).
For a complete list of television programs, consult the daily newspapers.

Public Transportation

The Downtown Transportation
Center, located at 300 N. Casino
Center Blvd. and Stewart Ave.,
serves as a transportation hub for
Citizens Area Transit (CAT) buses
and the downtown trolley. Most bus
lines connect to the center, as does
the trolley system. The center is
open daily 6:15 am-6:45 pm; holidays 6 am-6 pm. In addition to
ticket and route information personnel, the facility also has a restaurant.

*Strip Bus (702) 228-7433. 1-way fares
for routes 301, 302 and 303: adults, $2;
ages 62 and over, 6-17 and persons with
disabilities (with reduced-fare photo ID
card), $1. 1-way fares for all other routes:*

adults, $1.25; ages 62 and over, 5-17 and persons with disabilities (with reduced-fare ID), 60¢. Exact change is required. Tokens (called CAT Coins) or a monthly pass can be purchased at the Downtown Transportation Center. One easy way to travel from place to place on the Strip, or between the Strip and downtown, is to take the CAT bus. Twenty-four hours a day, the CAT bus (Route 301) runs at 10-minute intervals north and south along the Strip between the southernmost point, Vacation Village, and the northernmost point, the Downtown Transportation Center. The Strip Express (Route 302) runs this same route daily at 15-minute intervals from 10 am to 1 am.

Local residential bus service to several areas, including Henderson and Boulder City, is also available. Call for more information.

Downtown Trolley *(702) 229-6024. Fares: adults, 50¢; ages 62 and over, ages 17 and under and disabled, 25¢.* Shuttle buses designed to look like trolleys depart the Downtown Transportation Center daily every 20 minutes from 7 am to 11 pm. The route traveled is along Ogden Ave. (eastbound) to the Charleston Plaza Shopping Center and Fremont St. (westbound). The entire route takes 30 minutes to travel. (Do not confuse this trolley with the Strip Trolley.) See the *Downtown Las Vegas* map.

Strip Trolley *(702) 382-1404. Fare: $1.50. Exact change is required.* Like the Downtown Trolley, the Strip

Trolley also uses shuttle buses designed to look like trolleys. The trolley line operates daily 9:30 am to 1:30 am along Las Vegas Blvd. South, from the Mandalay Bay on the south end to the Stratosphere Tower on the north end. An additional loop includes the Las Vegas Hilton and a portion of Paradise Rd. The trolleys pass by each stop about every 15 minutes. (Do not confuse this trolley with the Downtown Trolley.) See the *Las Vegas Strip* map.

Taxi *$2.20 base fare plus $1.60 per mile; 35¢ per minute for standing still. Pickups at McCarran International Airport pay $1.20 tax per load.* For visitors who come to Las Vegas to enjoy gaming and entertainment, a convenient way of getting around is by cab. Taxis are plentiful, particularly at the entrances of the major resort hotels, and using them helps avoid the nuisance of having to find a parking space in a crowded lot. In addition, if two or three people share one taxi, it compares favorably to the cost of the bus, and there is usually no waiting. A typical trip half the length of the Strip will cost between $10 and $17; from the airport to the middle of the Strip, $10 to $12; and from the airport to downtown, $16 to $24.

Visitors who are staying at a hotel or motel not frequented by cabs or who wish to arrange for a taxi at a particular time may phone any of the following companies for service in Las Vegas. Upon request, ABC

Union, Ace, Nellis and Western provide vans with wheelchair lifts at regular taxi rates.

ABC Union/NLV (702) 736-8444

Ace   (702) 736-8383

Checker/Star/Yellow
                     (702) 873-2227

Desert   (702) 873-2000

Henderson   (702) 384-2322

Nellis   (702) 248-1111

Western   (702) 736-8000

Hospitals

Desert Springs Hospital
2075 E Flamingo Rd
Las Vegas
(702) 733-8800

Lake Mead Hospital Medical Center
1409 E Lake Mead Blvd
North Las Vegas
(702) 649-7711

St. Rose Dominican Hospital
102 E Lake Mead Dr
Henderson
(702) 616-5502

Sunrise Hospital and Medical Center
3186 S Maryland Pkwy
Las Vegas
(702) 731-8012

University Medical Center
1800 W Charleston Blvd
Las Vegas
(702) 383-2454

Valley Hospital Medical Center
620 Shadow Ln
Las Vegas
(702) 388-4863

AAA/California State Automobile Association

Office hours: Mon-Fri 8:30 am-5:30 pm

Henderson District Office
601 Whitney Ranch Dr, Ste A
Henderson
(702) 458-2323

Las Vegas District Office
3312 W Charleston Blvd
Las Vegas
(702) 870-9171

Summerlin District Office
8440 W Lake Mead Blvd, Ste 203
Las Vegas
(702) 360-3151

Visitor Services

Boulder City Chamber of Commerce
1305 Arizona St, Boulder City
(702) 293-2034
Office hours: Mon-Fri 9 am-5 pm

Las Vegas Convention and Visitors Authority
3150 Paradise Rd, Las Vegas
(702) 892-7575, 892-0711
Office hours: Mon-Fri 8 am-6 pm, Sat-Sun 8 am-5 pm

Nevada Welcome Center
100 Nevada Hwy, Boulder City
(702) 294-1252
Office hours: Daily 8 am- 4:30 pm

DOLPHIN HABITAT AND SECRET GARDEN—*See Mirage.*

ELVIS-A-RAMA MUSEUM *Behind the Fashion Show Mall at 3401 Industrial Rd. (702) 301-7200. Open daily 9 am-7 pm. Adults $9.95; seniors, $7.95.* From gold records to blue suede shoes, this museum displays the world's largest collection of Elvis memorabilia, including costumes, cars, movie posters, concert footage and contracts. Impersonators offer hourly tribute shows.

EXCALIBUR HOTEL & CASINO *3850 Las Vegas Blvd S. (702) 597-7777; (800) 937-7777. Dragon battle staged nightly on the hour, dusk-midnight.* This huge, castle-shaped hotel is themed throughout after the medieval days of King Arthur. Outside at the hotel's moat-style entrance, a fire-breathing dragon battles Merlin the magician nightly.

Fantasy Faire Midway *Motion-simulator theaters open Oct through May, Mon-Thu 10 am-10 pm, Fri-Sat 10 am-11 pm, Sun 9 am-10 pm. Extended hours Jun-Sep. $3 per person.* Among the attractions here are two motion-simulator theaters, medieval-themed midway games, strolling entertainers and the Court Jester's Stage, where performances take place throughout the day.

Tournament of Kings *Open daily; seatings at 6 and 8:30 pm. (760) 597-7600.* A Camelot-themed dinner show is performed while guests dine on a four-course meal consisting of soup, game hen, potato and a dessert. King Arthur, his sons Mordred and Chris, wizards, knights and fire-breathing dragons battle during the meal.

FREMONT STREET EXPERIENCE *Fremont St from 4th to Main sts in downtown Las Vegas. (702) 678-5600. Free nightly shows on the hour 8 pm-midnight.* The four blocks of downtown once known as "Glitter Gulch" have been transformed into a pedestrian-only zone covered by a 90-foot-high latticed canopy embedded with 2.1 million lights. Dubbed the Fremont Street Experience, this $70 million attraction features a 540,000-watt, high-tech, computer-controlled light and music show.

GAMEWORKS *In Showcase Mall, 3785 Las Vegas Blvd S. (702) 432-4263. Open Sun-Thu 10 am-midnight, Fri-Sat to 2 am. Hours may vary in summer. Game prices vary.* This virtual-reality arcade, created by Steven Spielberg, Sega Enterprises and Universal Studios, touts more than 200 video games of every description. Among the many attractions players can try their luck on are ski slopes, battlefields and raceways. The centerpiece is Surge Rock, a 75-foot-tall rock-climbing structure. The facility also maintains a full-service bar and food services.

GUINNESS WORLD OF RECORDS MUSEUM *2780 Las Vegas Blvd S. (702) 792-3766. Open daily at 9 am; Labor Day to Memorial Day to 5:30 pm, rest of year to 7:30 pm. Adults, $6; ages 62 and over, students and military, $5; ages 5-11, $4.* Rare videos and artifacts commemorate the world's fastest, greatest, rarest and richest feats from the worlds of entertainment, art, sports and science. Literally thousands of records can be accessed from the "Guinness World of Records" and "World of Sports" data banks. The "world" of Las Vegas is featured in a display highlighting the city's history, casinos and entertainers.

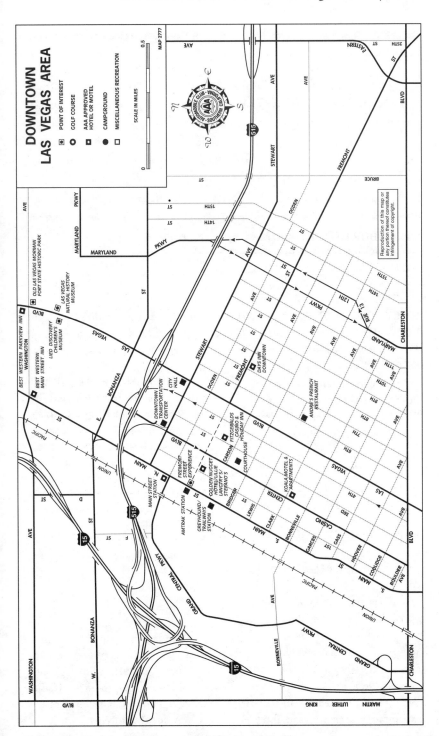

♠ Show Your Card & Save

Certain attractions offer AAA members a special discount. The discount is given to both adults and children, and applies to the member and his or her family traveling together, usually up to six people. The discount may not apply if any other gate reduction is offered or if tickets are purchased through an agent rather than the attraction's ticket office. Because such discounts change frequently, they are not listed here. For current information on such attractions and discounts, check the most recent edition of the AAA *Southern California & Las Vegas TourBook*. When in doubt, ask if a discount is available at the time of your visit.

HOLY COW CASINO, CAFE AND BREWERY *2423 Las Vegas Blvd S. (702) 732-2697. Open 24 hours. Free tours daily; call for schedule.* Opened in 1992 as Las Vegas' original microbrewery, Holy Cow uses traditional brewing methods and features several award-winning brews. Cow enthusiasts will appreciate the cow accents throughout the interior and the "cowlectibles" sold in the gift shop. The restaurant serves a variety of American-style fare.

IMPERIAL PALACE AUTO COLLECTIONS *Imperial Palace Hotel, 3535 Las Vegas Blvd S. (702) 794-3174. Open daily 9:30 am-9:30 pm. Adults, $6.95; ages 65 and over and 4-12, $3; ages 3 and under, free.* This auto museum, located on the fifth level of the hotel's parking structure, features more than 200 antique, classic and special-interest autos, antique trucks, motorcycles, and cars once owned by gangsters and world-famous celebrities. It also

houses one of the world's largest collections of Model J Duesenbergs. Vehicles are available for purchase.

LAS VEGAS ART MUSEUM *9600 W Sahara Ave. (702) 360-8000. Open Tue-Sat 10 am-5 pm, Sun 1-5 pm. Adults $5, seniors $3, students $2.* This 30,000-square-foot institution, which has a permanent collection of over 175 works, is an affiliate of the Smithsonian Institute and features exhibits drawn from the latter's behemoth cumulation.

LAS VEGAS CONVENTION CENTER *3150 Paradise Rd. (702) 892-0711.* With over 3.2 million square feet of meeting and exhibit space, the newly-expanded convention center—slated for completion late in 2001—is able to host some of the largest tradeshows anywhere. This $150 million facility offers 170 meeting rooms with seating capacities up to 7,500, as well as a 500-seat on-site restaurant.

The Imperial Palace Auto Collections feature changing exhibits of classic, antique and special-interest autos, trucks and motorcycles.

LAS VEGAS HILTON *3000 Paradise Rd.* This longtime Vegas flagship, once host to Elvis Presley's crowd-pleasing act, now draws fans of one of television's legendary shows.

Star Trek: The Experience *Open daily 11 am-11 pm. (702) 697-8700.*

- **Deep Space Nine the Promenade** *Free.* Characters made famous in the *Star Trek* television and film shows mingle with visitors to this dining and shopping experience, which includes five boutiques housing the largest collection of officially licensed *Star Trek* merchandise in the world. At Quark's Bar and Restaurant, the menu includes Romulan Ale (German pilsner), Glop on a Stick (corn dog) and The Wrap of Khan (chicken fajita wrap).

- **The Voyage Through Space** *$24.99; minimum height 42".* This 22-minute excursion to the 24th century starts on the bridge of the USS *Enterprise.* After boarding a shuttlecraft, a four-minute simulated space battle ensues. Victors exit to Deep Space Nine the Promenade. Admission to the History of the Future, a self-guided exhibit of more than 200 *Star Trek* costumes and props from movies and television programs, is included.

LAS VEGAS MINI GRAN PRIX *1401 N Rainbow Blvd. (702) 259-7000. Open daily at 10 am; Sun-Thu to 10 pm; Fri and Sat to midnight. Closed Dec. 25. $4.50 per ticket or $20 for 5. Must be 36" tall to ride Dragon roller coaster.* This motor-amusement center features racetracks where children and adults alike can test their driving skills. Vehicles range from "Kiddie Karts" and go-karts to sprint karts and Grand Prix vehicles.

LAS VEGAS MOTOR SPEEDWAY *7000 Las Vegas Blvd N. (702) 644-4444. Call for ticket prices and program information.* This racing complex hosts a wide range of events throughout the year on its 1.5-mile oval, most prominently the Las Vegas 400 NASCAR Winston Cup race each March. Several smaller tracks accommodate everything from drag racing to road-course events.

The Las Vegas Natural History Museum has one of the most complete exhibits of animated dinosaur replicas in the Southwest.

LAS VEGAS NATURAL HISTORY MUSEUM *900 Las Vegas Blvd N. (702) 384-3466. Open daily 9 am-4 pm. Adults, $5.50; ages 55 and over, students and military, $4.50; ages 4-12, $3; ages 3 and under, free.* The museum features an animated dinosaur exhibit, which includes a 35-foot *Tyrannosaurus rex*; an international wildlife room with mounted animals, including a giraffe; a 3000-gallon tank filled with live sharks; and a display of plants and wildlife native to Southern Nevada and the Southwest desert. Children may illuminate various animals in an African Savanna exhibit. There is also a gift shop on premises.

LIBERACE MUSEUM *2 miles E of the Strip at 1775 E Tropicana Ave. (702) 798-5595. Open daily to 5 pm; Mon-Sat from 10 am, Sun from 1 pm. Closed Jan 1, Thanksgiving and Dec 25. Adults, $8.95; ages 13-18, 60 and over and students, $5.95; ages 12 and under, free. Children must be accompanied by an adult.* The museum's collection of memorabilia, antiques and classic cars includes Liberace's million-dollar wardrobe and extensive fur collection, his gold and diamond stage jewelry and a Baldwin grand piano inlaid with thousands of etched mirror tiles. Of particular interest are a piano that Chopin once played and a crucifix presented to Liberace by Pope Pius XII. The recently expanded and renovated museum also displays Liberace's miniature piano collection, a photographic history of his life, and a recreation of his former office and bedroom.

LIED DISCOVERY CHILDREN'S MUSEUM

833 Las Vegas Blvd N. (702) 382-3445. Open Tue-Sun 10 am-5 pm. Closed Mon, except most school holiday Mon. Adults, $6; military, ages 55 and over and 1-17, $5; infants and museum members, free. Kids can really "live it up" at this unusual museum, which includes over 100 hands-on exhibits in the arts, humanities and sciences—if they like, they can pick a job, earn a paycheck, deposit it in a bank and shop for groceries. There's also a science tower and a weather station.

Lied Discovery Children's Museum features a number of intriguing exhibits for the younger set.

Eighteen rare and antique pianos are on display in the Piano Gallery at the Liberace Museum.

Mandalay Bay's Shark Reef lets visitors get up-close and personal.

LUXOR LAS VEGAS *3900 Las Vegas Blvd S. Recorded information (702) 262-4555.* From the massive sphinx outside to the elegant atrium lobby, this pyramid-shaped resort endeavors to make a visit to Egypt entirely unnecessary.

Pharaoh's Pavilion *Open daily 9 am-11 pm. IMAX shows screen daily; call for show times. Museum admission, $5. Show admission, $8.95. Tickets should be purchased 15 minutes in advance.* The Luxor's entertainment complex transports guests back in time to a replica of King Tut's Tomb and Museum, reconstructed to exacting detail; an audiotape-guide assists in exploring this self-paced tour. The seven-story high IMAX theater offers various two-and three-dimensional movies. In Search of the Obelisk is a motion simulator ride that explores a fictional underground civilization.

MANDALAY BAY RESORT & CASINO *3950 Las Vegas Blvd S. (877) 632-7000; (702) 632-7777.* With its 11-acre sand beach and its lush indoor foliage, this resort is designed to resemble an exotic tropical paradise. Colorful birds take flight in the high-ceilinged lobby; the gift shops and boutiques offer everything from imported rum to Balinese carvings.

House of Blues *Restaurant open daily at 8 am-11 pm. Nightclub open 11 pm-4 am. Club cover charge $10.* This restaurant/live-music venue has a huge collection of publicly displayed folk art. The restaurant features Southern-inspired cuisine and a traditional Sunday gospel brunch; the club offers live rock, and rhythm and blues music.

Shark Reef *Open daily 10 am-11 pm. Adults $13.95; ages 5-12, $9.95; ages 4 and under, free.* This new mini-aquarium features over 100 species of fish and reptiles from the world's tropical waters, including a dozen varieties of sharks. The main tank holds nearly 1.3 million gallons of water.

MGM GRAND HOTEL AND CASINO *3799 Las Vegas Blvd S, across from New York-New York. (702) 891-1111. Lion habitat open daily 11 am-10* *pm. Free.* A 45-foot tall, 100,000-pound bronze lion, perched atop a 25-foot pedestal, greets visitors and guests of the city's—and country's—biggest resort. The hotel features Art Deco decor and a Golden Age of Hollywood theme; among the Star Lane boutiques is an Emerald City Gift Shop offering *Wizard of Oz* memorabilia. The indoor Lion Habitat provides a showcase for public appreciation of the creatures, and permits lions to encircle guests via a see-through walkway tunnel that runs through the habitat.

THE MIRAGE *3400 Las Vegas Blvd S. (702) 791-7111. White Tiger Habitat open 24 hours. Free.* The longtime home of Siegfried & Roy's stage show features a Polynesian design and an indoor tropical rain forest. The Royal White Tigers of Nevada featured in the magic show are on view in the White Tiger Habitat, located on the hotel's southwestern side just off the casino. Street of Dreams is a winding boulevard of designer boutiques; Renoir is a chic dining room decorated with paintings by its namesake and other Impressionists.

Dolphin Habitat and Secret Garden *Open daily; Thu-Tue 11 am-5:30 pm; holidays from 10 am. Adults $10; ages 10 and under accompanied by an adult, free. Dolphin Habitat only (Garden closed) on Wed, $5.* A close look at seven Atlantic bottle-nose dolphins is the main draw of the Dolphin Habitat, which offers continuous 15-minute tours focused primarily on the facility's underwater viewing room. The Secret Garden features eight zoological environments with animals from the Siegfried & Roy show, which can be observed through a floor-to-ceiling wall of glass, while they sleep, eat and play.

The Volcano *Shows daily dusk-midnight. Free.* Located at the hotel's front entrance, the volcano's fiery, smoke-belching explosions occur every few minutes after dusk and never fail to momentarily stop traffic on the famous Strip.

NELLIS AIR FORCE BASE *Main gate at Las Vegas Blvd. and Craig Rd. (702) 652-1110.* Nellis, a weapons testing and tactical fighter training center, is also the home of the Thunderbirds, the Air Force's precision flying team. The Thunderbirds are often away performing at air shows throughout the country, but they do perform at the Nellis AFB Open House, which is held every two years; call for schedule.

Thunderbird Museum *Located on the base (directions given at main gate). (702) 652-4018. Tours discontinued until further notice. Call for current info.* The museum tour normally offered to the public features a short program, film and close-up look at an F-16 static display.

NEVADA STATE MUSEUM AND HISTORICAL SOCIETY *Located in Lorenzi Park; 700 Twin Lakes Dr. (702) 486-5205. Open daily 9 am-5 pm. Closed Jan 1, Thanksgiving and Dec 25. Adults, $2; ages 17 and under, free.* This lakeside museum has three galleries with permanent exhibits and one gallery that changes exhibits annually. Two of the permanent galleries focus on natural history and one focuses on the history of the Southern Nevada region. A research library is also located here. American Indian jewelry and books and videos about Nevada's history can be purchased in the museum store.

New York-New York Hotel & Casino, which opened in 1997,
is an example of the new wave of theme resorts to appear
along the Strip in recent years.

NEW YORK-NEW YORK HOTEL & CASINO *3790 Las Vegas Blvd S, across from MGM Grand.* *(702) 740-6969.* Contributing to the creation of Las Vegas' Manhattan skyline are several scaled landmarks, including the Empire State Building, the Chrysler Building, the Century Building, the CBS Building, the Statue of Liberty, and a 300-foot Brooklyn Bridge. Adding to the New York-style ambiance are an elegant Art Deco lobby, Greenwich Village and Little Italy—where visitors can purchase soft pretzels, Manhattan clam chowder, Italian-sausage sandwiches and, of course, New York-style pizza.

Coney Island Emporium *Open daily at 8 am, Mon-Thu to 2 am, Fri-Sun to 3 am.* This arcade re-creates an early 1900s atmosphere complete with old-fashioned midway games and attractions, as well as modern video games that feature the latest in high-tech gadgetry.

ESPN Zone *Open daily from 8 am, Mon-Fri to 1 am, Sat-Sun to 2 am.* This new sports-themed entertainment complex is comprised of the Sports Arena, which offers 10,000 square feet of interactive and competitive attractions; the Screening Room, which features multi-game viewing of televised games; and the Studio Grill, a restaurant with sports-themed artwork.

Manhattan Express *Open daily 10 am-11 pm, Fri-Sat to 11:30 pm. Admission.* Next to the emporium is the 203-foot-tall Manhattan Express roller coaster, which travels upside down and through part of the casino. Riders experience the world's first "heart line" twist and dive maneuver, which causes a momentary sensation of weightlessness.

OLD LAS VEGAS MORMON FORT STATE HISTORIC PARK

500 E Washington. (702) 486-3511. Daily 8 am-4:30 pm. Closed holidays. Adults, $2; ages 6-12, $1; ages 5 and under, free. This fort, built by Mormon settlers in 1855, is the oldest European-American building in the state of Nevada. It provided shelter for gold-seekers, emigrants and other travelers along the Spanish Trail/Mormon Road. At the turn of the 19th century, the fort was owned by the San Pedro, Los Angeles and Salt Lake Railroad (now part of Union Pacific); it also served as a resort, dairy and farm for the burgeoning new town of Las Vegas. Sections of the park have been renovated. In order to maintain the character of the fort, its walls have been reconstructed with parts reflecting a state of disrepair; a re-created stream flows along the same route as the park's original stream; and a pioneer demonstration garden has been planted. Historic photographs, interpretive panels and antiques from the mid-1800s are on display.

Paris Las Vegas offers a quaint shopping venue with cobblestone streets.

PARIS LAS VEGAS *Across from Bellagio, 3645 Las Vegas Blvd S. (702) 946-7000.* Famous architectural landmarks from Europe's City of Light create a Parisian environment, replete with a ⅖-scale Arc de Triomphe, facades of the Paris Opera House and the Louvre, as well as a replica of the Hotel de Ville.

Eiffel Tower *Open daily 9 am-1 am, weather permitting. Adults, $9; ages 65 and over, $7; ages 5 and under, free.* The real Eiffel Tower, built in France for the 1889 World's Fair, has been duplicated in ½ scale on the Las Vegas Strip, using Gustav Eiffel's original blueprints. A restaurant inside the superstructure is 100 feet above the Strip. Guests may also take a glass elevator to an observation deck on the 50th story.

Le Boulevard *Open daily 9 am-10 pm.* The authentic-looking French shopping venue modeled after the Rue de la Paix—complete with cobblestone streets and winding alleys—offers over 31,500 square feet of elegant boutiques and shops, including a bakery and a wine cellar, and eight restaurants.

RIO SUITE HOTEL & CASINO

3700 Flamingo Rd. (702) 252-7777. This off-Strip, Brazilian-themed resort has carved out a wild and colorful reputation for itself; the hotel's Club Rio and VooDoo Lounge are two of the most popular nightclubs in town.

Masquerade Show in the Sky *Thu-Tue; call for current operating hours. Viewing free; participation $9.95.* Floats suspended from the ceiling parade through the casino, bearing costumed performers who throw beaded necklaces to the crowd below. Guests can participate in the carnival-like activity.

Scandia Family Fun Center features all kinds of family fun, including three 18-hole miniature golf courses, bumper boats and a large video game arcade.

Masquerade Village *Open daily 9 am-10 pm.* This shopping mall captures the style and fun of New Orleans at Mardi Gras. The 26 boutiques and 6 restaurants are a mix of the upscale and the unusual.

SAM'S TOWN HOTEL & GAM-BLING HALL *5111 Boulder Hwy. (702) 456-7777. Free Strip shuttle.* This off-Strip, Western-themed hotel on the Eastern perimeter of the city features a 56-lane bowling center and an RV Park.

Sam's Town Mystic Falls Park *Water show daily at 2, 6, 8 and 10 pm. Free.* A nine-story atrium encloses this 25,000-square-foot indoor park, which houses lifelike animals, lush tropical foliage, waterfalls and meandering footpaths. Restaurants with patio seating, shops and the hotel itself surround the park. Featured is the Sunset Stampede, a 10-minute choreographed water show with laser lights.

SCANDIA FAMILY FUN CENTER
On the W side of I-15, S of Sahara Ave; 2900 Sirius Ave. (702) 364-0070. Jun through Sep open 24 hrs; Oct through May, daily from 10 am; Sun-Thu to 10 pm, Fri-Sat to 11 pm. Unlimited all-day wristband, $16.95; Supersaver all-attraction pass, $11.95; individual ride admissions $4.50. Unlimited golf, adults $6.95; children over 36", $5.95. The amusement center features three elaborate 18-hole miniature golf courses, go carts, bumper boats, baseball batting cages and a large video game arcade. Snack bar on site.

SOUTHERN NEVADA ZOOLOGI-CAL-BOTANICAL PARK *3 miles NW of downtown; 1775 N Rancho Dr. (702) 648-5955; 647-4685. Open daily 9 am-5 pm. Closed Jan 1, Thanksgiving and Dec 25. Adults, $5.95; ages 2-12 and 60 and over, $3.95.* Children will enjoy this limited zoological-botanical park, which exhibits a collection of mostly small animals and exotic birds. Featured are the last family of Barbary apes in the U.S., animals ranging from alligators to tigers, and all venomous reptiles found in Southern Nevada. Birds on display range from ravens and talking parrots to golden eagles and ostriches. A snack bar and gift shop are located on the grounds. Off-road tours of the surrounding desert area that includes the perimeter of "Area-51" are also available.

SPORTS CENTER *Located near McCarran International Airport; 121 E Sunset Blvd. (702) 317-7777. Call for hours. Individually priced attractions.* At this indoor/outdoor facility (formerly All-American SportPark), visitors may in-line or roller skate on an indoor floor, scale multiple graded routes on a climbing wall, bat home runs in batting cages that are designed like real baseball stadiums, race on NASCAR tracks designed by Jeff Gordon, play miniature golf or compete on high-tech video games.

STRATOSPHERE *2000 Las Vegas Blvd S. (702) 380-7777; (800) 998-6937. Open daily from 10 am; Sun-Thu to 1 am, Fri-Sat to 2 am. Call for prices and further information.* The focus of this landmark hotel is the Stratosphere Tower rising 1149 feet above the Strip. The tallest free-standing observation tower in the United States, it is 156 feet taller than the Eiffel Tower in Paris.

An eye-catching sight with its futuristic, Space Needle-like appearance and soaring height, it features two observation platforms, a revolving restaurant with 360-degree views, a cocktail lounge, meeting rooms and two thrill rides—the world's highest roller coaster, the High Roller, and an acceleration ride, the Big Shot. The Strat-O-Fair offers bumper cars and carnival games, while the Tower Shops promenade combines 45 boutiques with themed street scenes of Paris, New York and Hong Kong.

TREASURE ISLAND AT THE MIRAGE, *3300 Las Vegas Blvd S. (702) 894-7111.* This pirate-themed resort is distinguished by its colorful 18th-century village exterior, as carefully detailed as a movie set; inside, the hotel is designed to resemble a Caribbean hideaway.

This pirate ship at Treasure Island is the star of one of the best shows in town.

Buccaneer Bay *Shows daily at 4, 5:30, 7, 8:30, 10 and 11:30 pm. No performances during inclement weather or high winds; subject to last-minute cancellation. Arrive early for best viewing; standing room only. Free.* Located at the hotel's main entrance on the Strip, Buccaneer Bay treats passersby to a highly entertaining sea battle between an 80-foot-long pirate ship and a British frigate. The show features numerous fiery explosions, live actors and lots of witty, swashbuckling dialogue.

TROPICANA CASINO & RESORT
3801 Las Vegas Blvd S. (702) 739-2411, (800) 468-9494. This glitzy mainstay of the Strip is the home of the long-running *Folies Bergere.*

Casino Legends Hall of Fame *(702) 739-2222. Open daily 7 am-9 pm. Admission $4; children under 18 must be accompanied by an adult.* This 6000-square-foot exhibit space features some 15,000 items of memorabilia, including Liberace and Elvis costumes, old slot machines and historic photographs of Vegas.

UNIVERSITY OF NEVADA, LAS VEGAS
4505 S Maryland Pkwy. (702) 895-3011; campus tours (702) 895-3443. More than 23,000 students attend classes on the 335-acre campus. The university's curricula include courses in art and architecture, engineering, law, mathematics, science and many other subjects. The school, which opened in 1957, is home to a new $55 million high-tech research library. For campus tours, call or drop by the admissions office, Maude Frazier Hall, Room 114. A brochure for the self-guided arboretum tour of the campus is available from the UNLV News and Public Information Office, the Museum of Natural History and the grounds department.

Donna Beam Fine Art Gallery *In the Alta Ham Fine Arts Bldg, Rm 145-A. (702) 895-3893. Open Mon-Fri 9 am-5 pm, Sat 10 am-2 pm. Closed Sun and major holidays. Free.* The gallery hosts changing exhibitions by students, faculty and invited artists.

Flashlight *Between the Artemus W Ham Concert Hall and the Judy Bayley Theatre; N end of Academic Mall.* This striking 38-foot-high, 74,000-pound steel sculpture was fashioned by acclaimed artists Claes Oldenberg and Coosje van Bruggen.

Marjorie Barrick Museum of Natural History *On campus; E of Swenson St at end of Harmon Ave. Metered parking adj to museum. (702) 895-3381. Open Mon-Fri 8 am-4:45 pm, Sat 10 am-2 pm. Closed Sun and holidays. Free.* The museum encompasses permanent exhibits on the archaeology, geology and biology of the desert Southwest, an outdoor botanical garden, and taxidermy displays of indigenous animals.

Performing Arts Center *Adjacent to Maryland Pkwy; N end of Academic Mall. Schedule and ticket information (702) 895-3801. Tickets range in price from free to $75.* The center, comprised of the Artemus W. Ham Concert Hall, Judy Bayley Theatre and Alta Ham Black Box Theatre, regularly presents major international performing artists in classical and popular music, dance, theater and opera. It is also home to the Nevada Symphony Orchestra, Nevada Opera-Theatre and the Community Concert Association, whose seasons run from September through May and include professional

Strolling entertainers liven up the Grand Canal Shoppes at the Venetian.

performances in ballet, symphonic and chamber music, and opera.

Sam Boyd Stadium *Off campus; via US 93/95 (use Russell Rd exit) in Silver Bowl Regional Park. Ticket information (702) 895-3900.* The stadium is home to the university's NCAA football team, the Rebels, from September through November. It also hosts motocross competitions and concerts in the summer.

Thomas and Mack Center *Off Tropicana Ave at Swenson St. Events schedule and ticket information (702) 895-3900.* This 18,500-seat indoor arena hosts sporting events, concerts and shows. From November through February it is the home court for the school's NCAA Runnin' Rebels Mountain West basketball team.

THE VENETIAN RESORT HOTEL CASINO *3355 Las Vegas Blvd S. (702) 414-1000.* Full-scale replicas of Venice's most famous landmarks have been re-created at this resort, including the Ca D'Oro (Palace of Gold); St. Mark's Square, including its 315-foot Campanile Tower; the Bridge of Sighs; Doge's Palace, with Lady Justice who sits atop the palace; and the Rialto Bridge.

Gondola Rides *Offered daily 10 am-11 pm. Same-day reservation (beginning at 9 am) required in person at the loading dock in St Mark's Square. Adults, $10; ages 12 and under, $5. Cash only.* Gondoliers serenade visitors in Italian as they propel their guests up and down the canals traversing the Grand Canal Shoppes.

Grand Canal Shoppes *(702) 414-4500. Open Sun-Thu 10 am-11 pm, Fri-Sat to midnight.* A collection of international boutiques and specialty stores are featured in a Venetian streetscape, complete with strolling carnival characters and street performers who entertain

Surrounded by a stark desert landscape, Floyd Lamb State Park emerges as an oasis of tree-shaded groves and gentle beauty.

throughout the day. A small Houdini Museum features artifacts and memorabilia related to the illusionist.

Guggenheim Hermitage Museum *(702) 414-2440. Open daily 10 am-11 pm. Adults, $15.* Rotating exhibits of masterpieces from the collections of the Solomon R. Guggenheim Museum in Manhattan and the prestigious State Hermitage Museum in St. Petersburg, Russia, are shown in this new 7660-square-foot facility off the hotel's front lobby. Some 20 works from each collection are displayed at any one time.

Guggenheim Las Vegas *(702) 414-2440. Open daily 9 am-10 pm. Adults, $15.* This new 63,700-square-foot museum off the casino displays shows ranging from fashion and architecture exhibits to multimedia presentations and high-technology-based art. With 70-foot ceilings, the hangar-like space was designed to accommodate large-scale traveling exhibitions.

Madame Tussaud's Celebrity Encounter *Open daily 10 am-10 pm.*

Adults, $12.40; ages 4-12, $10; ages 65 and older and Nev residents, $10.75; ages 3 and under, free. Wax likenesses of more than 100 celebrities are exhibited in five themed-display areas, including Las Vegas legends Frank Sinatra, Dean Martin and Sammy Davis Jr., sports greats Babe Ruth, Arnold Palmer and Muhammad Ali, and Hollywood stars Elizabeth Taylor, Harrison Ford and Whoopi Goldberg.

THE VOLCANO—*See Mirage.*

WET 'N WILD *2601 Las Vegas Blvd S. (702) 734-0088. Open May through Sep, daily at 10 am; closing time varies. Admission, $25.95; ages 3 and under, $19.95; 55 and over, $14.95.* This 26-acre, family-oriented water park features Willy Willy, a hydra-hurricane ride; Lazy River, a 10-minute floating jaunt around the wave pool; and Der Stuka, a 76-foot-high water slide. In addition, there are rapids, a 500,000-

gallon wave pool, a surf lagoon and a children's pool. There are also areas for sunbathing and picnicking.

THE WYNN COLLECTION OF FINE ART *3145 Las Vegas Blvd. (702) 733-4100. Open daily 10 am-5pm. Adults $10; ages 5 and under, free.* This gallery off the lobby of the former Desert Inn houses the personal collection of hotelier Steve Wynn, whose new resort Le Rêve is slated to open on this site in 2004. Wynn provides commentary via audio wand on paintings by Picasso, Matisse, Gauguin, Manet, Pissarro and others.

North Las Vegas

See **A Quick Guide to Las Vegas** in this chapter under Las Vegas.

FLOYD LAMB STATE PARK *15 miles NW of Las Vegas off US 95, E at Durango; 9200 Tule Springs Rd. (702) 486-5413. Open daily 8 am-dusk. Closed Jan 1 and Dec 25. Entrance fee $5 per vehicle.* The park encompasses 2040 acres, including **Tule Springs Ranch**, four small lakes and the surrounding natural desert area. Fishing is permitted in all four lakes, which are stocked with rainbow trout in winter and catfish in summer. Largemouth bass live in the lakes, but the catch is low. Swimming, wading and boating are not allowed. Picnic tables and grills are located throughout the park and are available on a first-come, first-served basis. Self-guided hiking trails traverse tree-shaded groves and pass by the lakes.

The Tule Springs area has long been known as one of the best Pleistocene fossil sites in western North America. Remains found here have included giant sloths, bison, camels, horses and mammoths. Man's first presence in the area, however, only dates back 10,000 to 11,000 years, although today that presence is much more in evidence. The area that is now Floyd Lamb State Park was used as a watering stop by American Indians and local prospectors, and as a rest stop for horses on the Bullfrog Stage Line to Rhyolite. John Herbert Nay began farming the land in 1916, but sold it in 1928. The land remained vacant until 1941 when Jacob Goumond turned it into a working ranch.

When Nevada's divorce laws became the most liberal in the country by requiring only a six-week residency, Goumond saw a chance to make money with a "dude" ranch. Divorcees who came to live out their residency requirements occupied themselves with horseback riding, swimming, tennis, hayrides, barbecues, dances and a shooting range. But even as a dude ranch, Tule Springs remained a working farm. Livestock included a herd of cattle, dairy cows, horses, chickens, turkeys and pigs. Fruits and vegetables were grown year round and 100 acres were cultivated in alfalfa. Ranch denizens today include peacocks, ducks and geese. Visitors may roam the grounds of the old Tule Springs Ranch. A group of 22 historic structures are currently used only by park staff; future plans call for rehabilitation of the site. The buildings are identified in a park brochure, available at the entrance station.

GUIDED TOURS

The tours listed in this section generally last less than a day, though some of the trips to more distant places involve an overnight stay. Be sure to contact the companies in advance for complete information and reservations; many tours offer hotel pickup and discounted children's rates. Also, check refund policies to avoid losing your deposit in the event of a late cancellation. Scheduled tours are subject to cancellation if there is an insufficient number of passengers.

Tours listed are provided as a convenience for our readers; inclusion in this publication does not imply endorsement by the Automobile Club of Southern California.

Las Vegas

ADVENTURE PHOTO TOURS *3111 S Valley View Blvd, Ste X-106. (702) 889-8687, (888) 363-8687.* Grand Canyon, Hoover Dam, Red Rock Canyon, Spring Mountains NRA, Lake Mead, Valley of Fire State Park, Death Valley, Bryce Canyon and "Area-51" land tours.

AIR VEGAS AIRLINES *Henderson Executive Airport. (702) 736-3599, (800) 255-7474.* Grand Canyon.

ANNIE BANANIE'S WILD WEST TOURS *1824 Wincanton Dr. (702) 804-9755.* Valley of Fire, Lake Mead.

BALLOON LAS VEGAS *3675 S Rainbow Blvd, Ste 701-310. (702) 596-7582.* Las Vegas, Lake Mead hot air balloon tours.

♠ Grand Canyon Flights

In 1987 the U.S. Congress passed a law prohibiting flights below the canyon rim, and directed the National Park Service (NPS) and the Federal Aviation Administration (FAA) to designate safe routes for flights over the national park area. Congress also mandated that the NPS work to re-establish the "natural quiet" of the canyon. The NPS then proposed to the FAA that flight-free zones be established over 45 percent of the Grand Canyon, that air-tour operators be restricted to flying in specific routes over the least-used parts of the park, and that pilots be required to stay above the canyon rim. The law took effect in September 1988. A report, which evaluated both safety and noise pollution generated by park overflights, was submitted to Congress in 1994. The NPS and FAA are working together to develop a final use plan for the canyon that may restrict the number of flights and/or the noise level that the flights may generate. According to a government spokesperson, those flying over the canyon can still view much of the grandeur of the park. The main concerns are passenger safety and the noise level.

Flights over the region's national parks are popular with Las Vegas visitors.

DESERT ECO-TOURS *Southern Nevada Zoological-Botanical Park, 1775 N Rancho Dr. (702) 647-4685, 648-5955. Reservations required; age restrictions on some tours.* "Area-51," Colorado River, Rainbow Canyon, Cathedral Gorge, Lincoln County land tours.

DESERT STAR HOT AIR BAL-LOON ADVENTURES *9672 Marble Peak Ct. (702) 240-9007.* Las Vegas Valley.

GRAY LINE TOURS *Coach USA, 795 E Tropicana. (702) 644-2233.* Grand Canyon, Colorado River, Hoover Dam/Lake Mead, Valley of Fire/Lost City Museum of Archeology, Red Rock Canyon/Mount Charleston, Las Vegas, Laughlin land tours and air/land tours.

GUARANTEED TOURS *7440 S Industrial Rd, Ste 206. (800) 777-4697, (702) 369-1000.* Hoover Dam, Lake Mead, Death Valley, Valley of Fire, Red Rock, Las Vegas, Laughlin land tours; Grand Canyon, Bryce, Monument Valley air/land tours; river rafting, helicopter and Hummer tours.

KEY TOURS *3305 W Spring Mountain Rd, Ste 18. (702) 362-9355.* Hoover Dam, Laughlin and Primm land tours.

ROCKY TRAILS *(702) 869-9991, (888) 867-6259.* Grand Canyon, Zion, Death Valley, Valley of Fire, Red Rock land tours.

SHOWTIME TOURS OF LAS VEGAS *1550 S Industrial Rd. (702) 895-9976.* Grand Canyon, Hoover Dam, Las Vegas, Laughlin, Oatman air and air/land tours; river rafting and Hummer combo.

SIGHTSEEING TOURS UNLIM-ITED (STU) *4740 S Valley View. (702) 471-7155.* Grand Canyon, Hoover Dam, Lake Mead, Las Vegas, Laughlin, river rafting, off-road Hummer tours, air and land tours.

SUNDANCE HELICOPTERS, INC. *5596 Haven St. (702) 736-0606, (800) 653-1881.* Grand Canyon, Hoover Dam/Lake Mead and Las Vegas helicopter tours.

North Las Vegas

SCENIC AIRLINES *2705 Airport Dr. (702) 638-3300, (800) 634-6801.* Grand Canyon, Colorado River, Las Vegas, air tours; Bryce Canyon, Monument Valley air/land tour.

SHOWROOM ENTERTAINMENT

Headline entertainment is second only to gambling in the number of visitors it attracts to Las Vegas. The big showrooms typically feature a well-known singer or comedian backed by an opening act, or a glitzy revue with elaborate sets and costumes. While magicians, impressionists and Elvis impersonators abound, the latest trend is the importation of Broadway shows. Facilities listed here seat 500 or more.

Showroom listing does not imply AAA endorsement for the lodging establishment. For the most current information, refer to the Auto Club's Las Vegas Shows schedule, available to AAA members at all Southern California district offices, or the various entertainment guides available at the Las Vegas Convention and Visitors Authority and elsewhere.

Tickets for revues or production shows can be purchased by phoning or visiting the hotel's showroom box office or by contacting a local ticket agency. There are a number of ticket agencies in Las Vegas that specialize in booking entertainment. Refer to the telephone directory yellow pages under "Ticket Sales/Events" or "Tourist Information."

Many showrooms offer advance ticket sales and reserved seating. Be sure to ask at the time of purchase if the seats are reserved. If you have assigned seats, you should arrive approximately 20 minutes prior to show time. If seats are not assigned, then it is advisable to arrive at least an hour prior to curtain. Dinner shows may require even earlier arrival, although such options—once common—are disappearing.

Prices change frequently and without notice. While some hotels offer free afternoon lounge shows, sales tags for long-running revues and big-name headline acts have increased dramatically in recent years. Prices at press time ranged from $15 to $120, with an average of $50-60 per person, not

including taxes and gratuities; the numbers will often be raised for especially popular entertainers, as well as for opening and closing nights.

Large production shows often run indefinitely, many of them for several years. As of press time, shows scheduled to run indefinitely appear in the listings, but any show is subject to change without notice. You are advised to verify shows, times and prices in advance.

Although the early and late shows are basically the same in terms of content, children are generally not admitted to the late shows. The hour alone prevents most children from enjoying themselves, and entertainers feel freer to use language and discuss subjects that might not be appropriate for a general audience. For this reason, not only children but sensitive adults should attend the early shows. Production shows with nudity usually do not admit children; call the theater's box office in advance for any age restrictions that may apply.

Nightclubs and dance clubs have become an increasingly popular aspect

Elaborate stage productions entertain thousands of visitors with dazzling sets and beautiful dancers.

of Vegas' nightlife in recent years. Among the venues are the Luxor's Egyptian-themed dance spot, Ra; MGM Grand's trendy Studio 54, named for the renowned 1970s New York City club; Mandalay Bay's exotic rumjungle; the hip Club Rio at Rio Suites Hotel; and the state-of-the-art C2K at the Venetian. Many of the clubs have dress codes.

Las Vegas

ALADDIN RESORT & CASINO
3667 Las Vegas Blvd S. (702) 736-7114.

Aladdin Theater for the Performing Arts—Top-name entertainment and production shows. *Times and prices vary.*

BALLY'S LAS VEGAS *3645 Las Vegas Blvd S. (702) 967-4567.*

Jubilee Theater—*Donn Arden's Jubilee! (Indefinitely). Sat-Thu 7:30 and 10:30 pm. Dark Fri. Admission. Minimum age 18.*

BELLAGIO *3600 Las Vegas Blvd S. (702) 693-7111, (888) 987-6667.*

Bellagio Theatre—*O starring Cirque du Soleil (Indefinitely). Fri-Tue 7:30 and 10:30 pm. Dark Wed and Thu. Admission. Tickets can be purchased 90 days in advance.*

FLAMINGO LAS VEGAS *3555 Las Vegas Blvd S. (702) 733-3333, (800) 221-7299.*

Flamingo Showroom—Top-name entertainment. *Times and prices vary with entertainers.*

HARD ROCK HOTEL AND CASINO *4455 Paradise Rd. (702) 693-5066.*

The Joint—Top-name entertainment. *Times and prices vary with entertainers.*

Siegfried & Roy have a lifetime contract at the Mirage.

HARRAH'S-LAS VEGAS *3475 Las Vegas Blvd S. (702) 369-5111.*

Harrah's Showroom—*Clint Holmes (Indefinitely). Mon-Sat 7:30 pm, Thu and Sat also 10 pm. Dark Sun. Admission. Also production shows.*

IMPERIAL PALACE *3535 Las Vegas Blvd S. (702) 794-3261.*

Imperial Theatre—*Legends in Concert (Indefinitely). Mon-Sat 7:30 and 10:30 pm. Dark Sun. Admission; age 1 and under free. Smoke-free theater.*

LAS VEGAS HILTON *3000 Paradise Rd. (702) 732-5755.*

Hilton Theater—Top-name entertainment. *Times and prices vary with entertainers.*

LUXOR LAS VEGAS *3900 Las Vegas Blvd S. (702) 262-4400, 288-1000.*

Luxor Theater—*Blue Man Group: Live at Luxor (Indefinitely). Wed-Mon 7 and 10 pm. Dark Tue. Admission.*

MANDALAY BAY RESORT & CASINO *3950 Las Vegas Blvd S. (877) 632-7400.*

Mandalay Bay Events Center—Top-name entertainment. *Times and prices vary with entertainers.*

Storm Theater—*Storm (Indefinitely). Sun, Mon, Thu 7:30 pm; Fri 10:30 pm; Wed, Sat 7:30 and 10:30 pm. Dark Tue. Admission.*

MGM GRAND HOTEL AND CASINO *3799 Las Vegas Blvd S. (702) 891-7777, (800) 929-1111.*

EFX Theatre—*EFX Alive (Indefinitely). Tue-Sat 7:30 and 10:30 pm. Dark Sun and Mon. Admission.*

Hollywood Theatre—Top-name entertainment. *Times and prices vary with entertainers.*

MGM Grand Garden Arena—Top-name entertainment/special events. *Times and prices vary with entertainers.*

THE MIRAGE *3400 Las Vegas Blvd S. (702) 791-7111, (702) 796-9999.*

Danny Gans Theatre—*Danny Gans (Indefinitely). Tue-Thu and Sat-Sun 8 pm. Dark Mon and Fri. Admission.*

Siegfried & Roy Theatre—*Siegfried & Roy at the Mirage (Indefinitely). Sun-Mon 7:30 pm. Tue and Fri-Sat 7:30 and 11 pm. Dark Wed-Thu. Admission. Minimum age 5. Tickets can be purchased 90 days in advance.*

MONTE CARLO RESORT & CASINO *3770 Las Vegas Blvd S. (702) 730-7160, (877) 386-8224.*

Lance Burton Theatre—*Lance Burton, Master Magician (Indefinitely). Tue-Sat 7 and 10 pm. Dark Sun-Mon. Admission.*

NEW YORK-NEW YORK HOTEL & CASINO *3790 Las Vegas Blvd S. (702) 740-6815.*

Broadway Theater—*Michael Flatley's Lord of the Dance (Indefinitely). Tue-Wed 7 and 10 pm; Thu-Fri 9 pm; Sat 3 and 8 pm. Dark Mon. Admission.*

A surreal moment in Cirque du Soleil's Mystère *at Treasure Island.*

THE ORLEANS *4500 W Tropicana Ave. (702) 365-7075.*

Orleans Showroom—Top-name entertainment. *Times and prices vary with entertainers.*

PARIS LAS VEGAS *3645 Las Vegas Blvd S. (702) 946-4567.*

Le Theatre des Arts—Top-name entertainment. *Times and prices vary with entertainers.*

RIO SUITE HOTEL & CASINO *3700 Flamingo Rd. (702) 252-7777, (888) 746-7784.*

Copacabana Showroom—*Scintas* (Indefinitely). *Fri-Tue 8 pm. Tue 10:30 pm. Dark Wed-Thu. Admission.*

Samba Showroom—Top-name entertainment and production shows. *Times and prices vary with entertainers.*

RIVIERA HOTEL AND CASINO *2901 Las Vegas Blvd S. (702) 794-9433.*

La Cage Theater—*An Evening at La Cage* (Indefinitely). *Wed-Mon 7:30 and 9:30 pm. Dark Tue. Admission. Dinner options available.*

Splash Theatre—*Splash* (Indefinitely). *Nightly 7:30 and 10:30 pm. Admission. Minimum age 18.*

SAHARA HOTEL *2535 Las Vegas Blvd S. (702) 737-2515.*

Congo Room—*The Rat Pack is Back!* (Indefinitely). *Mon and Wed 6:30 and 9 pm; Tue and Fri-Sun 8 pm. Admission. Dinner options available.*

STARDUST HOTEL *3000 Las Vegas Blvd S. (702) 732-6325, (800) 824-6033, ext 6325.*

Wayne Newton Theatre—The singer alternates with other top-name entertainment. *Times* and prices vary with entertainers.

STRATOSPHERE *2000 Las Vegas Blvd S. (702) 380-7711, (800) 998-6937.*

Broadway Showroom—*American Superstars* (Indefinitely). *Sun-Tue 7 pm; Wed and Fri-Sat 7 and 10 pm. Dark Thu. Admission. Dinner package available.*

Viva Las Vegas (Indefinitely). *Mon-Sat 2 and 4 pm. Dark Sun. Admission.*

TREASURE ISLAND AT THE MIRAGE *3300 Las Vegas Blvd S. (702) 894-7711, (800) 392-1999.*

Treasure Island Showroom—*Mystère* starring Cirque du Soleil (Indefinitely). *Wed-Sun 7:30 and 10:30 pm. Dark Mon-Tue. Admission. Tickets can be purchased 90 days in advance.*

TROPICANA CASINO & RESORT *3801 Las Vegas Blvd S. (702) 739-2411, (800) 468-9494.*

Tiffany Theatre—*The Best of the Folies Bergere* (Indefinitely). *Fri-Wed 7:30 (all audiences) and 10 pm (topless). Dark Thu. Admission. Minimum age 16 (late show).*

The Illusionary Magic of Rick Thomas (Indefinitely). *Daily 2 and 4 pm. Dark Fri. Admission. Minimum age 5.*

THE VENETIAN RESORT HOTEL CASINO *3355 Las Vegas Blvd S. (702) 414-1000.*

Showroom at the Venetian—*Melinda, First Lady of Magic* (Indefinitely). *Thu-Tue 8:30 pm. Dark Wed. Admission.*

*On your mark, get set, go! Runners take to the streets in the
Las Vegas International Marathon.*

ANNUAL EVENTS

Parades, rodeos, art fairs, fireworks displays and golf tournaments
are just a few of the many annual community events that Las Vegas
and environs have to offer. For detailed information about each
event, please call the telephone numbers shown, or consult with the
local chamber of commerce or visitor information bureau. In addition, casino tournaments take place throughout the year. In Las
Vegas, spectator sports range from boxing to baseball, soccer to football and basketball to hockey.

Spectator sports are popular
throughout the year in the Las
Vegas area. The Las Vegas 51s baseball
club (702-386-7200), affiliated with
the Los Angeles Dodgers, plays its
home games at Cashman Field April
through September. The Thomas &
Mack Center is the home of UNLV's
NCAA Mountain West basketball
team, the Runnin' Rebels (702-895-
3900), who play November through
February. Sam Boyd Stadium is the
home venue for Rebels university football; the season runs September
through November.

Auto racing is a fast-growing sport at
the Las Vegas Motor Speedway, which
hosts the Las Vegas 400 NASCAR race
in March and many other events
throughout the year. For more information, call (702) 644-4444. Other
exciting sporting events throughout
the year include WBA and WBC boxing matches at the Las Vegas Hilton,
Caesars Palace, Mandalay Bay and
MGM Grand hotels.

Casino tournaments in bridge, blackjack, slot play, craps, poker, gin
rummy and bowling take place in

many casinos. Anyone interested in these tournaments should contact the hotel or venue directly for dates and play information; room reservations should be made well in advance, as room space is often at a premium during a tournament.

February

LAS VEGAS INTERNATIONAL MARATHON *(702) 240-2722.* The full marathon has been run every year since 1967, and the half-marathon since 1993. The half-marathon starts in Sloan, Nev., the full marathon in Jean, Nev.; running concurrently on the same path, both finish at Sunset Park in Las Vegas. Each event attracts more than 4000 participants from all 50 states and more than 35 countries.

April

NATIVE AMERICAN ARTS FESTIVAL *Clark County Museum, Henderson, Nev. (702) 455-7955.* American Indian food and art, dancing, craft demonstrations and storytelling are featured during this three-day festival.

HENDERSON HERITAGE DAYS *Various locations, Henderson, Nev. (702) 565-8951.* This 10-day event celebrates Henderson's heritage with a beauty pageant, live music, chili cookoff, talent show, car show, softball tournament, parade, 5-K run, and charity basketball tournament.

LAS VEGAS SENIOR CLASSIC *Tournament Players Club, Summerlin, Nev. (702) 242-3000.* This event is a three-day Senior PGA Tour tournament.

May

ARTFEST *Convention Center, Henderson, Nev. (888) 278-3378.* This two-day outdoor event features over 200 artists displaying their work and more than two dozen entertainment acts on three stages, plus a children's art workshop.

September

LAS VEGAS MARIACHI FESTIVAL *Mandalay Bay Events Center, Las Vegas, Nev. (800) 637-1006.* This day-long mariachi festival features top-name entertainers and bands, and is one of the most prestigious of its kind in the U.S.

HENDERSON EXPO *Sunset Station, Henderson, Nev. (702) 565-8951.* This three-day event features a new car show and carnival.

October

INVENSYS CLASSIC AT LAS VEGAS *Tournament Players Club in Summerlin, and TPC at The Canyons, and Southern Highlands Golf Club, Las Vegas. (702) 242-3000.* This PGA Tour event (formerly the Las Vegas Invitational Golf Tournament) lasts five days.

LAS VEGAS JAYCEES STATE FAIR *Las Vegas Motor Speedway, Las Vegas, Nev. (702) 457-8832. Sometimes held in Sep.* Livestock exhibits, a carnival midway and crafts booths are featured at this four-day event.

RENAISSANCE FAIRE *Sunset Park, Las Vegas, Nev. (702) 455-8273.* Historical reenactments, jousting, theatrical performances, food and strolling minstrels highlight this two-day event.

December

CHILDREN'S CHRISTMAS PARADE *Water St, Henderson, Nev. (702) 565-8951.* Held on a Saturday, this parade features floats, horses and a visit from Santa Claus.

NATIONAL FINALS RODEO *UNLV's Thomas & Mack Center, Las Vegas, Nev. (702) 895-3900.* This professional rodeo event takes place over 10 days and features saddle bronco, bareback and bull riding; calf roping; steer wrestling; and barrel racing.

NEW YEAR'S EVE CELEBRATIONS *Various locations. (702) 892-7575.*

The National Finals Rodeo brings PRCA events to the Thomas & Mack Center at UNLV.

Outside Las Vegas

*From the grandeur of Hoover Dam to the pine forests of Mount Charleston, a world of opportunity beckons those who venture beyond the lures of Las Vegas. Most of the surrounding region remains undeveloped, with a host of opportunities awaiting the adventurous traveler. To the southeast of Las Vegas is **Boulder City**, a tidy town that has maintained its down-home, historic atmosphere. The town serves as gateway to Hoover Dam and the many diversions of **Lake Mead National Recreation Area**. For breathtaking desert views, head west to **Red Rock National Conservation Area** or northeast to **Valley of Fire State Park**, both within an hour's drive of the Strip. Close as well is **Spring Mountains National Recreation Area**, home of Mount Charleston, the third-highest peak in Nevada; it's less than an hour's drive to the northwest. At the California-Nevada border, the tiny town of **Primm** has emerged as a family entertainment center. Thanks to the Desperado roller coaster and other thrill rides, this former drive-through hamlet has become a tourist destination in its own right.*

POINTS OF INTEREST

Attractions are listed alphabetically by city or area—**Boulder City, Lake Mead National Recreation Area, Overton, Primm, Red Rock Canyon National Conservation Area, Spring Mountains National Recreation Area** and **Valley of Fire State Park**. Listings of attractions located on hotel properties do not necessarily imply AAA approval of the lodging facilities.

See **A Quick Guide to Las Vegas and Vicinity** in the *Las Vegas Valley* chapter for information on the areas included in this chapter.

Boulder City

BOULDER CITY HISTORIC DISTRICT *23 miles SE of Las Vegas via US 93/95 on US 93/Nevada Hwy. Chamber of Commerce located at 1305 Arizona St. (702) 293-2034.* Boulder City was created to house the thousands of workers who built nearby Hoover Dam. It also takes a place in American history as this country's first fully developed, master-planned community. Listed on the National Register of Historic Places, Boulder City provides a glimpse into an earlier era, an oasis of Americana in the vast Southern Nevada desert.

Among Boulder City's many historic buildings, visitors will encounter numerous parks, generous landscaping, wide avenues lined with vintage street lamps, and charming, well-kept homes. Interestingly, this community of about 15,000 is also the only city in Nevada where gaming has always been, and still is, illegal.

The construction of Boulder City began in 1931 and continued nonstop for nearly two years. While the rest of the country struggled during the Great Depression, this sparkling new community thrived—the population swelled to more than 8000 while the dam was being built. At that time Boulder City was the third-largest city in Nevada.

Through the 1940s, Boulder City flourished as a regional government center and tourism point for the dam and Lake Mead. The community remained under the jurisdiction of the federal government, however, ensuring its proper development under the original plan. It took an act of Congress for Boulder City to become an incorporated municipality. The act passed and was signed on July 9, 1958, and Boulder City was incorporated on January 4, 1960.

A self-guided tour of the Boulder City Historic District is outlined in a brochure available at the local chamber of commerce. The historic district is divided into five major areas, including parks and public buildings, three residential sections and a commercial district. The city's best-known historic structure and focal point is the **Boulder Dam Hotel**, a pine-shingled, Dutch Colonial-style building on Arizona Street. Built in 1933 to accommodate a growing tourist industry, the 33-room hotel was Southern Nevada's finest inn, boasting private baths and showers in each room—a rarity for the times—and an elegant lobby paneled in rare southern gumwood. The hotel hosted a steady stream of Hollywood celebrities, American politicians, European aristocrats and Far Eastern royalty. The newly-renovated Boulder Dam Hotel is the home of the Boulder City Chamber of Commerce, the Boulder City/Hoover Dam Museum, and the Boulder City Arts Council and Art Gallery.

The Boulder Dam Hotel preserves the atmosphere of an earlier era.

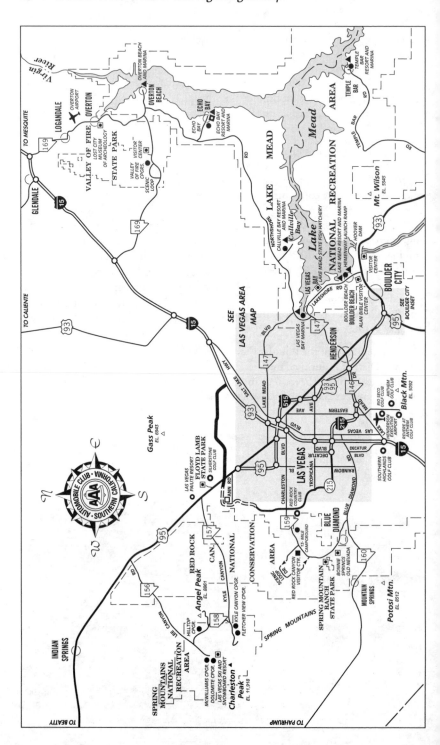

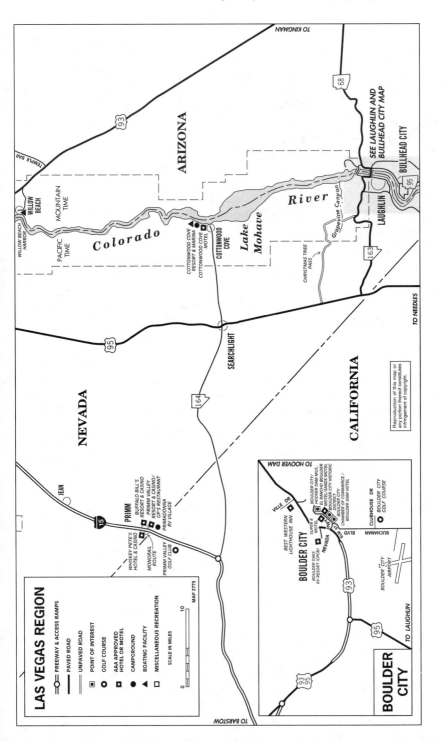

The 726-foot-high Hoover Dam is considered one of the engineering wonders of the world.

BOULDER CITY/HOOVER DAM MUSEUM *1305 Arizona St. (in Historic Boulder Dam Hotel). (702) 294-1988. Open daily to 5 pm; Mon-Sat at 10 am, Sun at noon. Sun hours may vary in summer. Closed Jan 1, Thanksgiving and Dec 25. Admission, $2; ages 16 and under and ages 65 and older, $1.* This small museum exhibits Hoover Dam-related artifacts, including a display of a dam workers' tent-house and a variety of historical photographs.

HOOVER DAM *30 miles SE of Las Vegas via US 93/95 on US 93. (800) 634-6787, (886) 291-8687. Guided tours daily 8:30 am-5:15 pm. Closed Thanksgiving and Dec 25. Admission, $10; ages 62 and over, $8; ages 7-16, $3; ages 6 and under, free. Hardhat tour (minimum age 7), $25. Free parking on Ariz. side; Nev. side, $3 per vehicle. Note: Due to security concerns, access to and tours of Hoover Dam may be restricted. Call for current status.* This 726-foot-high dam is a National Historic Landmark and considered one of the engineering wonders of the world. Built during the Great Depression with the skill, long hours and dedication of thousands of construction workers, it was completed in 1935—two years ahead of schedule. Not only did the dam help control the sometimes violent Colorado River, but it provided a cheap source of electricity, which aided the development of Las Vegas and Southern California. As an additional bonus, the dam created Lake Mead, America's largest man-made reservoir and a popular recreation spot.

In 1995, a $123-million visitor center and five-story parking structure opened to the public. The three-level visitor center features an exhibit gallery, revolving theater and observation platform. Two high-speed elevators operate daily to lower visitors 520 feet into the walls of Black Canyon for a 35-minute tour of the dam's power plant; a one-hour hardhat tour provides a "behind-the-scenes" view of the structure's inner workings. For all visitors, the view from the bottom of Hoover Dam is awe-inspiring, leaving no doubt that this structure is truly an engineering marvel.

Lake Mead National Recreation Area

LAKE MEAD *25 miles SE of Las Vegas.* **Alan Bible Visitor Center** *located 4 miles NE of Boulder City on US 93. (702) 293-8990, 293-8906. The visitor center is open daily 8:30 am-4:30 pm. Closed Jan 1, Thanksgiving and Dec 25. The 6 major recreation areas on Lake Mead are* **Boulder Beach**, *28 miles SE via US 93 and SR 166;* **Las Vegas Bay**, *17 miles E via SR 147/Lake Mead Blvd;* **Callville Bay**, *29 miles E via SR 147, Northshore and Callville Bay rds;* **Echo Bay**, *54 miles NE via SR 147, Northshore Rd and access road to Echo Bay;* **Overton Beach**, *60 miles NE via I-15 and SR 169; and* **Temple Bar**, *in Ariz, 75 miles SE via US 93 and Temple Bar Rd. For emergency assistance in the Lake Mead National Recreation Area call (800) 680-5851 or (702) 293-8932 (911 is not fully implemented in the Lake Mead NRA).*

Effective May 2000, Lake Mead NRA assesses entrance and lake-use fees. Fees may be paid at greeter locations in the recreation area. Entrance fees: 1-5 days—$3 per person by foot or bicycle, $5 per vehicle; annual pass—$20 per vehicle. Lake-use fees (charged in addition to the entrance fee): 1-5 days—$10 for first vessel, $5 each additional vessel; annual pass—$20 for first vessel, $10 each additional vessel.

Lake Mead is the largest manmade reservoir in the United States. It is administered by the National Park Service as part of the Lake Mead National Recreation Area, which also includes Lake Mohave, downstream from Hoover Dam. Lake Mead is 110 miles long and has a shoreline five times that length. Created by Hoover Dam, the lake area offers year-round fishing, swimming, water-skiing, camping, hiking, picnicking, scuba diving, sailing, powerboating and houseboating. Information about the recreation area can be obtained at the Alan Bible Visitor Center on US 93, which also has a botanical garden, bookstore and exhibits on natural history.

Much of Lake Mead's surrounding landscape is rugged desert interspersed with stark grayish-purple mountains, colorful red rock canyons and a variety of desert shrubberies. Mild weather throughout most of the year is punctuated by hot, dry summers, when temperatures often reach over 100 degrees. The desert environment is home to more than 1000 bighorn sheep that roam the rocky ridges, while the manmade lake attracts ducks, cormorants, geese, egrets, herons, ospreys and bald eagles.

The lake offers some of the best sport-fishing in the country and an open season on all fish year round (see Water Recreation in the *Recreation* chapter). There are many **scenic drives** through this dramatic region. A popular one follows Northshore Road, running north from Lake Mead Boulevard (SR 147) to Echo Bay and Overton Beach. An often spectacular view of the surrounding mountains and hills can be seen from this route, where the browns, burnt reds and black rocks of the landscape are contrasted with the stark off-whites and tans. Each hill is seemingly formed from a different material, but all are the product of an active geologic past.

The red and black rocks that dominate the scenery speak of the high iron and magnesium content of the volcanic debris. Local sedimentary rocks, such as the sandstone layers evidenced in the nearby hills, were laid down by water and then uplifted at a later time.

A high iron content is also evidenced there, often by an entire range of stark red hills. The vividness of the colors of the rocks seen on this drive can often vary not only with the time of day, but also with the direction of travel. What may appear dull and drab through the front windshield may look entirely different in the rearview mirror. Drive carefully—one of the greatest hazards here is looking at the landscape instead of the road.

Caution: Care should be taken when traveling in this area.

- Desert thunderstorms in summer and fall can produce both lightning and flash floods. Never camp in a wash or low-lying area. Never drive across flooded roads; many roads have been posted flash-flood areas.

- Summer's extreme temperatures can cause heat exhaustion and heat stroke, as well as cripple a car that does not have adequate coolant in the cooling system. (Refer to the Desert Driving Hints in the *Transportation* chapter.)

- Poisonous snakes and scorpions are indigenous to this area. They usually will not strike unless cornered, but caution should be taken to avoid them.

- Drive only on paved roads or on unpaved roads marked with yellow arrows. Check with rangers about road conditions before traveling unpaved roads.

LAKE MEAD STATE FISH HATCHERY *9½ miles N of Boulder City on SR 166/Lakeshore Rd. (702) 486-6738. Open daily 8 am-4 pm. Free.* This facility is a cold-water hatchery used for trout. Its visitor center features displays on production methods.

LAKE MOHAVE *Extends 67 miles N from Davis Dam along the Colorado River. For general information call (702) 293-8990; for Lake Mohave weather call (702) 297-1265. Ranger stations can be found at the 3 major recreation areas on the lake:* **Katherine Landing**, *6 miles N of Bullhead City via SR 95, SR 68 and N on an access road; (928) 754-3272.* **Cottonwood Cove**, *55 miles N of Laughlin via Laughlin Cutoff Rd., SR 163, US 95 and an access road E from Searchlight; (702) 297-1265. Willow Beach, 81 miles N of Bullhead City via SR 95, SR 68 to Kingman, US 93 N and an access road W; (928) 767-4000.*

Lake Mohave's teal waters provide a sharp contrast to the desert landscape surrounding it. Its northern section is almost as narrow as the Colorado River itself, with Indian petroglyphs etched on the steep walls of Black Canyon. The midsection widens to almost four miles before narrowing again to the south, where the shore is lined with hundreds of small coves and inlets.

The contrast of the water to the desert is also reflected in the colorful flora and fauna. The lake is an abundant source of water for traditional desert dwellers, as well as a winter home for many migratory bird species. Homes for Gila monsters, scorpions, tarantulas, burros and coyotes, as well as small beavers, muskrats and bighorn sheep, can be found in the area. Birds run the gamut from hawks and large crows to roadrunners and blue heron. Spring often brings a display of wildflowers (most notably brittlebush and sand verbena) among the desert plants.

Lake Mohave is ideal for boating year round, but those pursuing land adventures will find the best months to visit are October through April. Winters are mild, with daytime temperatures generally ranging from 65 to 85 degrees. Brutally hot summer days are routinely above the 100-degree mark and sometimes reach 120 degrees.

The lake's main appeal is in the variety of recreation it offers. Houseboating and fishing are popular, as are swimming, scuba diving, water-skiing, windsurfing and sunbathing. Houseboats can be rented at Katherine Landing and Cottonwood Cove marinas, but reservations must be made well in advance. A fish hatchery at Willow Beach supplies the rainbow trout that are planted in the lake. Lake Mohave has a reputation as one of the best trout and largemouth bass fishing areas in the Southwest.

Overton

LOST CITY MUSEUM OF ARCHEOLOGY *60 miles NE of Las Vegas via I-15 and SR 169; 721 S Moapa Valley Blvd. (702) 397-2193. Open daily 8:30 am-4:30 pm. Closed major holidays. Adults, $2; ages 18 and under, free.* This museum offers visitors a chance to see both original American Indian relics and faithful reconstructions of Pueblo dwellings. The last 10,000 years have seen several cultures in residence, including the Gypsum Cave People, ancient Basket Makers, early Pueblos and, most recently, the Paiute Indians, who came to the area about 900 years ago. Many ruins near the museum have not yet been excavated, and as the delicate process of unearthing the remains continues, more and more is revealed about the area's past inhabitants.

Faithful reconstructions of Indian pueblo dwellings can be found at the Lost City Museum of Archeology in Overton.

Primm is the site of a growing number of attractions.

Primm

Located 40 miles S of Las Vegas at the California/Nevada state line on I-15. **Buffalo Bill's Resort & Casino, Primm Valley Resort & Casino** *and* **Whiskey Pete's Hotel & Casino** *(702) 382-1212, (800) 386-7867. Rides per person: Roller coaster, $6; Turbo Drop, $5; log ride, $4; motion theater, $5; virtual reality roller coaster, $5; all-day wrist bands are available, call for details. Rides subject to periodic closure.* This area, quite literally at the California-Nevada state line, was once just a drive-through hamlet on the way to bigger and better things. It was popularly known as State Line for several years. Today, however, Primm is itself a high-wattage destination, offering entertainment, lodging, dining and gaming at three large, resort-style hotels.

At Buffalo Bill's Resort & Casino, one of tallest and fastest roller coasters in the world, **Desperado**, offers thrilling rides around the entire property and into the casino itself. The roller coaster plunges 225 feet and reaches speeds of 80 mph while riders glimpse spectacular views of the surrounding desert. Additional thrills can be had on the **Turbo Drop**, which lifts riders 200 feet above the desert and sends them down at 45 mph before bouncing gently on air brakes. A little tamer, but just as fun, is the **Water Flume Log Ride**, which crisscrosses the path of the roller coaster and finishes with a gentle ride through the casino. Bill's is also home to a **virtual reality roller coaster.**

A **Western-style train** links Buffalo Bill's to Primm Valley, where in-between knocking down turkeys (three consecutive strikes) at the regulation bowling center, visitors can view an ornamental 100-foot **Ferris wheel** and a **merry-go-round.** Primm Valley also touts a 21,000-square-foot **convention center.**

From Primm Valley, a sleek, futuristic-looking monorail whisks passengers over I-15 to Whiskey Pete's. The hotel displays two classic gangster cars near the monorail terminal: the original

Bonnie and Clyde "Death Car" as well as the restored **Dutch Shultz-Al Capone Gangster Car.** Other items on display are gruesome in nature and may be upsetting to children and sensitive adults.

Visitors to Primm will also find relaxing activities such as a round of golf at the **Primm Valley Golf Club,** which offers two 18-hole championship courses. (See Golfing in the *Recreation* chapter.).

Red Rock Canyon National Conservation Area

18 miles W of Las Vegas via SR 159/W Charleston Blvd or 20 miles W of Las Vegas via SR 160/Blue Diamond Rd. **Visitor center** *located to the left of the scenic loop drive entrance; Bureau of Land Management, Red Rock Canyon NCA (702) 363-1921. Open daily 8 am-4:30 pm. Closed Jan 1, Thanksgiving and Dec 25. Entrance fee: $5 per vehicle; bicyclists and pedestrians, free.*

Just a short drive from the man-made wonders of Las Vegas, Red Rock Canyon features nature at its best: a 13-mile scenic loop drive, more than 20 miles of hiking trails, horseback riding, numerous panoramic overlooks, a variety of flora and fauna, American Indian rock art, plus a well-stocked visitor center with exhibit rooms and a bookstore. Picnicking sites are located at Red Spring and Willow Spring.

Because Red Rock Canyon is higher in elevation than Las Vegas (up to 5000 feet) and has double the annual rainfall (about 8 to 12 inches), a wider variety of plant and animal life is able to flourish here. Cacti, annuals, yucca (such as the Joshua tree) and trees (ponderosa and piñon pines, juniper and willow) are prevalent, as are many types of birds, such as hawks, eagles, falcons, roadrunners, owls, ravens and wrens. Many other birds migrate through during the spring and fall; the visitor center staff can provide a complete list.

Much of the wildlife in Red Rock is visible only during the early morning and late evening hours, when cooler temperatures prevail. Night-dwellers include mule deer, coyotes, mountain lions, badgers, bobcats, jackrabbits and bats. Easier-to-spot diurnal inhabitants are bighorn sheep, wild burros, wild horses and antelope ground squirrels (identified by their white tails).

Reptiles are no strangers to the area, and include tree frogs, geckos, lizards and snakes. There are also three types of poisonous rattlesnakes here, namely the sidewinder, Mojave green and Mojave speckled. Hot days (above 70 degrees) bring out snakes; use caution when hiking. And remember, all animals (including snakes) are protected at Red Rock Canyon.

The **Scenic Loop Drive** is a convenient way to view the beauty of Red Rock Canyon; the road is located just off SR 159 and open daily from 6 am to dusk. This one-way, 13-mile route begins near the visitor center, then returns to SR 159 about two miles farther south. The drive offers a close look at the area's Aztec sandstone, plant life and the **Keystone Thrust Fault.** The fault occurred some 65 million years ago and is considered the most significant geologic feature of Red Rock Canyon. It is believed

The beauty of Red Rock Canyon is easy to appreciate via the Scenic Loop Drive.

that two of the Earth's crustal plates collided with such force that part of one plate was shoved up and over the younger sandstone. The thrust contact is evidenced by the sharp contrast between the gray limestone and the red sandstone.

The first two pullouts on the scenic loop have short trails to the base of the **Calico Hills**, where seasonal rain pools can be found. These pools often become temporary homes to small insects, insect larvae and fairy shrimp. Easier hiking can be found a little farther along the drive at the **Sandstone Quarry** (a short, graded dirt road leads to this spot). From the historic quarry, many small canyons can be explored. A side road leads to the Willow Spring Picnic Area and a ⁹⁄₁₀-mile hike from the road takes visitors to **Lost Creek Canyon**, the site of a year-round spring and occasional seasonal waterfall.

Farther along the gently curving drive is **Ice Box Canyon Overlook**. From this location, visitors can take a ⅛-mile hike to a box canyon surrounded by steep walls; the walls keep this canyon cooler than others in the area—hence the name. The end of the hike is reached by "boulder hopping" an additional ½ mile across the canyon bottom. Seasonal pools and an occasional waterfall can also be found here. The last stop along the road is the **Pine Creek Canyon Overlook**, one of the area's most popular hiking trails. The two-mile round trip features a running creek, ponderosa pines and the remains of a historic homestead.

The scenic loop drive is also an excellent way for experienced **bicyclists** to see the area. The one-way paved road assures riders of no oncoming traffic, and since the road is two lanes wide, there is plenty of room for cars to pass.

Bicyclists will, however, find the road a bit of a challenge. Its steep, undulating grades gain 1000 feet in altitude over the first five miles, followed by switchbacks at the top of the grade, then by a 1000-foot drop in elevation over the last eight miles. Round-trip mileage is about 15 miles. Bicyclists should beware of weekend and holiday traffic, which can be heavy, and keep a lookout for falling rocks in the switchbacks, and loose pebbles and debris where the road crosses a wash. Since there is no repair facility or air for tires available in the park or in nearby Blue Diamond, cyclists should come prepared to make their own repairs. The visitor center has a brochure detailing the route.

Safety Guidelines:

• Thunderstorms, especially in summer and early fall, can produce both lightning and flash floods. Never drive across flooded roads or cross low-lying areas when water is running.

• Charcoal fires are allowed at designated sites where grills are provided. Ground fires are prohibited.

• Camping is permitted only in designated locations.

• Climbing on sandstone requires equipment and experience. Sandstone is soft and crumbly and can be dangerous to climbers.

• Heat, cold and dehydration can take their toll on hikers. Carry one gallon of water for each person per day. Summer days can bring extreme heat, and temperatures drop rapidly at night.

• All natural and historic features are protected by federal law. This includes animals, plants, rocks and American Indian artifacts. Do not damage, disturb or remove them.

• Do not feed the burros at Red Rock Canyon. Feeding burros encourages them to congregate on the roads, where many have been killed or injured by vehicles. Burros have also been known to bite, kick and step out in front of cars unexpectedly. Use caution and observe them from a distance.

BONNIE SPRINGS OLD NEVADA
Off SR 159/W Charleston Blvd., 5½ miles S of the Red Rock Canyon Visitor Center; 1 Gun Fighter Ln. (702) 875-4191. Open daily at 10:30 am; during daylight-saving time to 6 pm, standard time to 5 pm; tickets sold till 1 hour before closing. Petting zoo open daily at 10 am; during daylight-saving time to 6 pm, standard time to 5 pm. Train operates Sat, Sun and holidays only. Admission to Old Nevada: adults, $6.50; ages 62 and over, $5.50; ages 5-11, $4; train rides and petting zoo, free. In the 1800s Bonnie Springs Ranch was a stopover for wagon trains traveling the Old Spanish Trail. In 1952, Al and Bonnie Levinson built a replica of an old Western town here and fashioned it into a tourist attraction. Free activities include the petting zoo and rides on a miniature train. The petting zoo has donkeys, pigs, llamas, deer, a variety of other farm animals and a duck pond; food to feed them can be purchased from on-site vending machines. For a fee, visitors can experience the Old Nevada Village, a Western-style town that offers staged gunfights and hangings, a melodrama, wax museum, blacksmith display, stagecoach rides, horseback rides and more. A Western-themed motel, gift shop, restaurant and saloon are also on the premises.

SPRING MOUNTAIN RANCH STATE PARK *S of Scenic Loop Dr off SR 159, 15 miles W of Las Vegas via Charleston Blvd. (702) 875-4141; summer theater information (702) 594-7529. Day-use area open 8 am-dusk. Visitor center/ranch house open daily 10 am-4 pm. Closed Thanksgiving and Dec 25; call for holiday hours. Daily 45-min guided tours of the historic area; call for schedule. Gift shop open Wed-Sun 10 am-4 pm. Entrance fee: $5 per vehicle.* This 520-acre park at the base of the majestic Wilson Cliffs overflows with tranquil beauty. Listed on the National Register of Historic Places, during the 1830s the area was a welcome oasis for weary travelers on the alternate route of the Old Spanish Trail. Through most of the 20th century the site was used as a cattle ranch, changing ownership several times (including with Howard Hughes), before coming under park protection in 1974. Tours of the historic site and its circa-1860s structures are given throughout the year. A large, grassy day-use area, shaded by scrub oak and mesquite trees, is available for picnickers; tables and barbecue grills are provided. The park hosts many activities, including art shows, plays and musicals, at its outdoor theater June through August, and living history programs in the spring and fall.

Spring Mountains National Recreation Area

*35 miles NW of Las Vegas via US 95, turnoff at SR 157/Kyle Canyon Rd or SR 156/Lee Canyon Rd. **Visitor center (Las Vegas)** 4 blocks W of Sahara Blvd at 2881 S Valley View Blvd, Ste 16. (702) 873-8800. Open Mon-Fri 8 am-4:30 pm. Visitor center closed Sat, Sun and holidays (NRA open). **Visitor center (Kyle Canyon)** at Mile Marker 3 on SR 157. (702) 872-5486. Open Mon-Fri 10 am-3 pm, Sat-Sun 9 am-4 pm.* Barely a 45-minute drive from the glitz of Las Vegas is **Spring**

Joshua trees line the entrance to Spring Mountain Ranch State Park.

Spring Mountains National Recreation Area offers snow sports in the winter and a lush reprieve from high desert temperatures in the summer.

Mountains National Recreation Area. Part of the Humboldt-Toiyabe National Forest, Spring Mountains NRA provides a lush reprieve from high temperatures and stark landscapes of the desert. By taking the Spring Mountains Scenic Loop, visitors are exposed to a number of appealing sights as the road climbs to its maximum elevation of 8500 feet. At this elevation, the temperature in the forest is usually 30 degrees cooler than in Las Vegas. Weekend crowds attest to the forest's popularity; weekdays are usually quieter.

Caution: Portions of the national forest may close for the winter as early as October (depending on weather conditions), and tire chains may be required at any time during winter months. Gasoline is not available on the mountain.

Cathedral Rock, Old Mill, Foxtail and Deer Creek are enjoyable picnic spots. Another feature to look for is Mummy Mountain, so named because it looks like a huge mummy lying on its back. Restaurant dining with outdoor seating is available near Cathedral Rock. Hikers should bring comfortable walking shoes in order to experience the area's beauty up close; numerous hiking trails offer broad vistas and interesting flora and fauna.

Charleston Peak is the third-highest peak in Nevada. A trail to the 11,918-foot summit is usually open between June and October, though weather conditions can lengthen or shorten the hiking season considerably. Hikers should be in good condition before attempting the climb; the gain in elevation from start to finish is almost 4000 feet, and the total round trip is more than 18 miles.

LAS VEGAS SKI AND SNOWBOARD RESORT *47 miles NW of Las Vegas via US 95 and SR 156/Lee Canyon Rd. (702) 385-2754. Open Thanksgiving to Easter, daily 9 am-4 pm.* Rentals (alpine skis, boots and poles, snowboards), snowmaking, night skiing (depending on snow conditions), ski school, snack bar and day lodge are all available. Runs are 20 percent novice, 60 percent intermediate and 20 percent advanced, with the longest run being ⅗ mile. The vertical drop is 1000 feet. Three double chairs service the area; prices vary, call for information. The nearest AAA-approved accommodations are in Las Vegas. Remember that tire chains may be required when driving in this area.

Valley of Fire State Park

50 miles NE of Las Vegas via I-15 and SR 169 (Valley of Fire Rd) near Overton. (702) 397-2088. Entrance fee: $5 per vehicle. Camping fee: $12 per vehicle (includes entrance fee). Visitor center located just off Valley of Fire Rd, midway into the park. Open daily 8:30 am-4:30 pm. Closed Dec 25. So named because of the effect of bright sunlight reflecting off red sandstone, Nevada's oldest state park is a visually stunning area that contains dozens of unique geological formations and remnants of an ancient American Indian civilization.

During the dinosaur age 150 million years ago, these great sandstone formations were created from shifting sand dunes and years of uplifting, faulting and erosion. Prehistoric inhabitants of the area included the Basket Maker people, and later, Ancestral Puebloan farmers from the nearby Moapa Valley.

Nevada's oldest state park offers countless natural formations, brilliantly red in color, and all different shapes and sizes. Located near the east entrance station is **Elephant Rock**, one of the most photographed formations in the park; it resembles an elephant's profile when viewed from the hill behind, looking toward Valley of Fire Road. **Seven Sisters**, another striking formation, is also easily visible from Valley of Fire Road; it is just east of the visitor center. **The Beehives**, weathered by wind

Elephant Rock is one of the most photographed formations in Valley of Fire State Park.

and water, are near the west entrance station. The remnants of petrified logs are also within in the park, although thoughtless visitors have taken so many samples that the amount of petrified wood is considerably depleted.

For examples of **petroglyphs**—pictures carved into rock—**Atlatl Rock** is one of the best. Situated near the center of the park along Scenic Loop Road, the petroglyphs of the towering rock are easily viewed by walking up a steep, metal staircase. Visitors who brave the 83 mesh-covered steps to the top will be rewarded with the sight of ancient, well-preserved figures carved into the rock. Another site known for its petroglyphs is **Mouse's Tank**, a natural basin named after an early renegade who used the area as a hideout. Water collects in the rock after a rainfall, occasionally remaining in the tank for months.

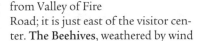

A climb to Atlatl Rock is richly rewarded with close-up views of Indian petroglyphs.

Because of its rare beauty, Valley of Fire has been used many times as the background for motion pictures. There are numerous hiking trails, as well as camping and picnicking facilities. The visitor center has an outdoor botanical garden, displays of local fauna, and information about the park and its hiking trails.

Caution: Care should be taken when traveling in this area.

- Thunderstorms, especially in summer and early fall, can produce both lightning and flash floods. Camp only in designated areas and never drive across flooded roads.

- All natural and historic features are protected. This includes animals, plants, rocks and American Indian artifacts. Do not damage, disturb or remove them.

- Care should be taken when hiking in canyon areas. Taking shortcuts may be dangerous. Never hike alone. Register at the visitor center before hiking backcountry areas. No overnight backpacking.

GUIDED TOURS

The tours listed in this section generally last less than a day, though some of the trips to more distant places involve an overnight stay. Be sure to contact the companies in advance for complete information and reservations, including deposit requirements and cancellation notice; scheduled tours are subject to cancellation if there is an insufficient number of passengers. Many tours offer hotel pickup and discounted children's rates.

Tours listed are provided as a convenience for our readers; inclusion in this publication does not imply endorsement by the Automobile Club of Southern California.

Boulder City

BLACK CANYON RAFT TOURS *1297 Nevada Hwy. (800) 696-7238, (702) 293-3776. Operates Feb through Nov. Closed Jan and Dec. Reservations advised.* Colorado River raft trips from Hoover Dam to Willow Beach.

COLORADO RIVER TOURS *205 Rainier Ct. (702) 293-4422, 291-0026.* El Dorado Canyon land tours (oldest gold mine in Nevada); Colorado River kayak and canoe trips and rentals.

LAKE MEAD AIR *1301 Airport Rd. (702) 293-1848, 293-9906.* Grand Canyon, Hoover Dam/Lake Mead air and air/land packages.

LAKE MEAD CRUISES *(702) 293-6180. Reservations recommended.* Lake Mead stern-wheeler cruises depart from Lake Mead Cruises Landing. Sightseeing, dinner/dance and breakfast cruises.

SHOWROOM ENTERTAINMENT

Primm's showrooms, while not as pervasive or as elaborate as those in Las Vegas, still add a noteworthy dimension to this growing tourist destination.

Tickets for shows may be purchased by phoning or visiting the hotel's showroom box office or by contacting a local ticket agency, of which there are a number that specialize in booking entertainment. Refer to the telephone directory yellow pages under "Ticket Sales/Events" or "Tourist Information."

Showroom listing does not imply AAA endorsement for the lodging establishment. For the most current information, refer to the Auto Club's Las Vegas Shows schedule, available to AAA members at all Southern California district offices.

Primm

Located along I-15 at the California-Nevada state line, this emerging area offers production shows, special events and lounge entertainment. Times and prices vary with entertainers.

BUFFALO BILL'S RESORT & CASINO *On E side of I-15. (702) 386-7867, (800) 386-7867.*

Star of the Desert Arena—Top-name entertainment. *Times and prices vary with entertainers.*

WHISKEY PETE'S HOTEL & CASINO *On W side of I-15. (702) 386-7867, (800) 386-7867.*

Whiskey Pete's Showroom—Top-name entertainment. *Times and prices vary with entertainers.*

ANNUAL EVENTS

The Boulder City area plays host to a number of annual events, while Logandale, more than 50 miles northeast of Las Vegas, hosts the Clark County Fair each year. For detailed information about each event, please call the telephone numbers shown, or consult with the local chamber of commerce or visitor information bureau.

April

CLARK COUNTY FAIR *Clark County Fairgrounds, Logandale, Nev. (702) 398-3247.* This four-day event features livestock shows, pony rides, arts and crafts booths, a PRCA rodeo and carnival rides.

May

SPRING JAMBOREE & CRAFT FAIR *Bicentennial Park, Boulder City, Nev. (702) 293-2034.* A two-day arts and crafts fair, classic car show, food booths and music are all part of this springtime festival.

July

DAMBOREE *Central Park, Boulder City, Nev. (702) 293-2034.* This old-fashioned Fourth of July celebration includes a parade, games, children's activities, live music, a carnival and fireworks.

September

RATTLIN' RAILS HANDCAR RACES *Yucca St Rail Yard, Boulder City, Nev. (402) 294-0982.* Five-person teams from as far away as Canada compete in different categories over two days, racing handcars down a pair of railroad tracks. A barbecue and awards ceremony follow the races.

October

ART IN THE PARK *Bicentennial Park, Boulder City, Nev. (702) 294-1611.* With arts and crafts on display in more than 300 booths, this two-day show is the largest of its kind in the western United States.

December

CHRISTMAS PARADE *Boulder City, Nev. (702) 293-2034.* A Saturday night parade down the Nevada Highway, ending at Bicentennial Park, helps celebrate the holiday season.

PARADE OF LIGHTS *Lake Mead. (702) 293-2034 (Boulder City, Nev.).* Boats ranging in size from 16 to 34-plus feet long gather on the nation's largest manmade lake to ring in the Christmas season with an evening's blaze of festive, twinkling lights.

Laughlin-Bullhead City

*Ninety miles south of Las Vegas are the booming towns of **Laughlin, Nevada**, and **Bullhead City, Arizona**. Perched on opposite banks of the Colorado River, they lack the vibrant atmosphere of Las Vegas, although Laughlin alone draws more than 4 million tourists annually. The town's relaxed pace, bargain-priced lodging and meals at its riverside hotel-casinos, and big band music attract the seniors. Popular music of the '70s, '80s and '90s draws baby-boomers to the lounges and showrooms. And some 10,000 to 15,000 "snowbirds" migrate from colder climes each year to make the area their winter home.*

Moreover, the region boasts many worthwhile attractions, ranging from hiking trails to historic mining towns, notably Oatman, Arizona. And of course, there's abundant recreation on the Colorado River.

POINTS OF INTEREST

Attractions are listed alphabetically. **Note**: The State of Arizona does not observe daylight-saving time; Mountain Standard Time is in effect year round.

COLORADO BELLE HOTEL & CASINO *In Laughlin at 2100 S Casino Dr. (702) 298-400. Cyber Roller Coaster runs daily at 9 am; Sun-Thu to 10 pm, Fri-Sat to 11 pm. $5 (42" height requirement).* This resort-casino is a striking 608-foot replica of a Mississippi paddle-wheel riverboat. It features nautically-themed hotel rooms, themed restaurants, a microbrewery, a 100-game video arcade and the Cyber Roller Coaster, a virtual-reality ride.

COLORADO RIVER MUSEUM *In Bullhead City, AZ, on SR 68 ¼ mile N of the Laughlin Bridge. (928) 754-3399. Open Sep through Jun, Tue-Sun 10 am-4 pm (Ariz time); . Closed holidays, Jul, Aug. Donation.* Housed in a former Catholic church built in 1947 during the Davis Dam construction, this small museum features a model of Fort Mohave in the late 1800s, geologic maps of the area, a model railroad that depicts the mid-1800s, and historical photographs. Items donated to the museum include a steamboat anchor, mining tools, antique barbed wire, American Indian artifacts, a dinosaur footprint, and a piano that was shipped around Cape Horn 140 years ago.

DAVIS CAMP COUNTY PARK *In Bullhead City, AZ, on SR 95 ½ mile N of the Laughlin Bridge. (928) 754-7250. Open till dusk; Mar 15-Oct 15 at 6 am; rest of year at 7 am. $3 entrance fee, $5 holiday weekends; $4 launching fee Mar 15-Oct 15.* The park offers a stretch of sandy beach for swimming and fishing, or launching personal watercraft, inner tubes, rafts or rubber boats. The area from the park north to Davis Dam is noted for its excellent striped bass and rainbow trout fishing. Visitors have found that a hike into the park's south section can provide views of a variety of birds and small wildlife. Camping is permitted (RVs only, no tents) along the river (see *Campgrounds & Trailer Parks*); fishing requires a license (see Water Recreation under *Recreation*).

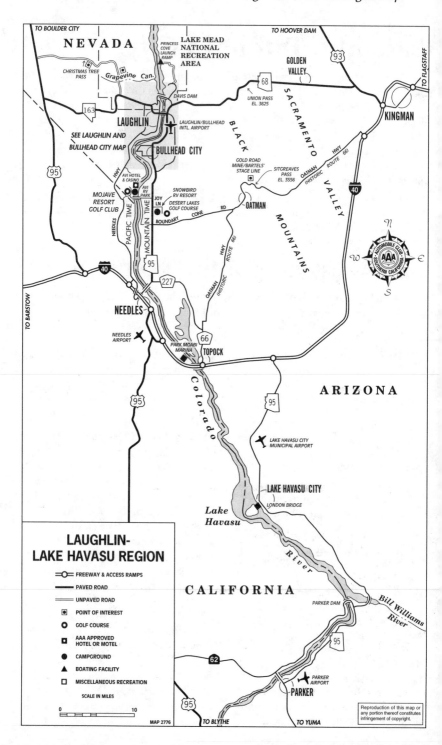

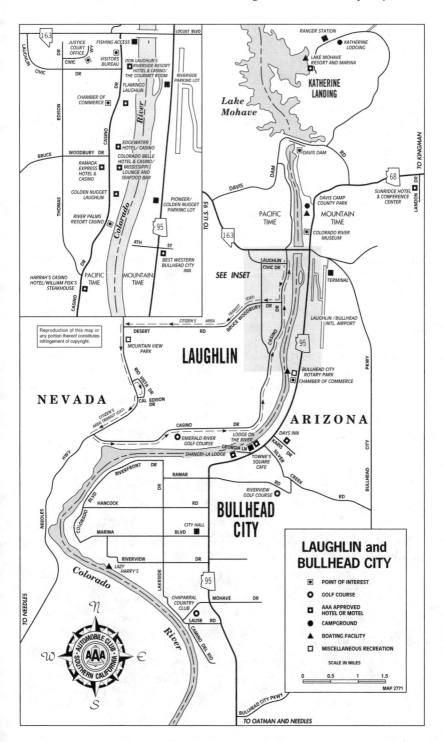

DAVIS DAM *2 miles N of Laughlin via Casino Dr and SR 163. (928) 754-3628.* The dam, designed to help regulate the delivery of water to the lower Colorado River region and Mexico, is a rock-fill and earthen structure augmented by concrete intakes and spillways. In addition to its importance for flood control, the dam provides hydroelectric power for regional industry and irrigation for farming. The powerhouse is no longer open for tours, but the dam can still be viewed up close.

DON LAUGHLIN'S RIVERSIDE RESORT HOTEL & CASINO *In Laughlin at 1650 S Casino Dr.*

Don Laughlin's Classic Car Collection *(702) 298-2535, ext 5678 or 5103. Open daily at 9 am; Mon-Fri to 10 pm, Sat-Sun to 11 pm. Free.* The collection features antique, classic and futuristic "concept" automobiles from the Imperial Palace in Las Vegas and Don Laughlin's private collection. The cars are exhibited in two rooms: a glass-walled room facing Casino Drive, and the Exhibition Hall on the third floor of the hotel's 26-story tower.

Don's Kid Kastle *(702) 298-2535, ext 5191; (800) 227-3849. Open daily at 10 am; Sun-Thu to 11 pm, Fri-Sat to midnight. Nursery open (ages 3-24 months) Sun-Thu 4-9 pm; Fri-Sat 2-10 pm. $6 an hour per child. Maximum daily stay is 5½ hours. Meals served at noon and 7 pm; $2.* Children ages 3 months to 12 years may stay at this facility. Activities include group play, nonviolent video games, and a giant castle where children may climb, slide and explore.

Riverside Lanes *(702) 298-2535, ext 5160, (888) 590-2695. Open 24 hrs; call for lane availability and prices. Cosmic Bowling, Wed 10 pm-midnight and Sat 9 pm-1 am. First come, first served.* The bowling center's 34 lanes feature automatic scoring and include two lanes that are equipped with Bowler Track, a system that shows the ball's motion from approach to release. Wednesday and Saturday nights during Cosmic

River boat shuttles offer a refreshing commute between Laughlin casinos.

Several Laughlin hotels boast their own boat docks.

Bowling the facility is illuminated with black lights and equipped with glow-in-the-dark pins and balls. Running lights, along the sides of the lanes, help bowlers aim at the incandescent pins.

U.S.S. *Riverside (702) 298-2535 ext 5770, (800) 227-3849 ext 5770. Departs from Don Laughlin's Riverside boat dock. Ticket booth located on the ground level of the hotel, next to boat dock.* Boat tours of the Laughlin-Bullhead City area and Davis Dam. Weddings held aboard.

GRAPEVINE CANYON/CHRIST-MAS TREE PASS *7 miles W of Davis Dam on SR 163 (about 6 miles W of Casino Dr), N on dirt access road (a small sign indicates the turn). (928) 754-3272. No restrooms or drinking water available.* This canyon offers excellent viewing of American Indian rock carvings of animals, fertility symbols and spiritual signs. These petroglyphs, which vary in age from 150 to more than 600 years old, are reached by a half-mile path from the parking area. Hikers will travel along the edge of a wash to a small incline in the canyon.

Heading north from the Grapevine Canyon parking lot (toward US 95) leads to Christmas Tree Pass, which gets its name from the piñon and juniper trees that locals have decorated with ribbons, plastic lids, paper and other bits of "trash" for many years. About four miles out of Grapevine Canyon the wide, graded dirt road narrows considerably to allow access for only one car in each direction; this section is not recommended for RVs. As the road leaves Christmas Tree Pass it widens out again for another five miles to US 95. **Note:** This road is subject to heavy washout during periods of rain.

Four-wheel-drive enthusiasts will find several backcountry roads that the National Park Service has approved for public access. They lead to secluded coves on the lake or into the desert mountain backcountry. It is advisable to check with the ranger for information about road conditions. *Caution:* Flash flooding can occur during inclement weather and sudden summer thunderstorms. Watch for unfenced mine shafts and pits. Stay out of abandoned mines; deep shafts, rotten timbers, and flammable or poisonous gases can be concealed inside the tunnels.

♠ *A Quick Guide to Laughlin-Bullhead City*

Population

Bullhead City   29,315

Laughlin   8,100

Elevation

Bullhead City   540 ft.

Laughlin   510 ft.

Emergency   911

Highway Conditions

Arizona   (888) 411-7623

Nevada   (702) 486-3116

Time/Weather

Arizona   (520) 763-3000

Nevada time   (775) 844-1212

weather   (702) 248-4800

Emergency Road Service for AAA Members

(800) AAA-HELP

(in the USA and Canada)

(800) 464-0889

(for the hearing impaired)

Newspapers

The Laughlin-Bullhead City area's daily newspapers are the *Mohave Valley Daily News* and the *Arizona Republic*. The major weeklies are the *Bullhead City Bee*, the Weekender and the *Laughlin Nevada Times*.

Radio Stations

For a complete list of radio programs, consult the daily newspapers.

Classic Rock: KLUK (97.9 FM); **Contemporary Rock**: KZUL (95.3 FM), KZZZ (100.3 FM); Country: KFLG (102.7 FM and 1000 AM), KGMN (104.7 FM), KWAZ (97.9 FM); **News/Talk:** KATO (1230 AM); **Oldies:** KRCY (105.9 FM).

TV Stations

In Laughlin, the major television stations include channels 3 (NBC), 5 (FOX), 8 (ABC) and 13 (CBS). In Bullhead City, Ariz., the major network programs appear on channels 5 (CBS), 10 (FOX), 12 (NBC) and 13 (ABC). For a complete list of television programs, consult the daily newspaper or hotel listings.

Public Transportation

Shuttles and Ferries—All of the hotels in Laughlin have large on-site parking lots. A water taxi runs between the casino docks at the Riverside, Edgewater, Pioneer, Golden Nugget and Harrah's; the fare is $1 one way and $2 round trip. On those occasions when the water level of the river (controlled by Davis Dam) is too low for the taxis to travel safely, parking lot pickups are made by shuttle buses.

In addition, Citizen Area Transit (CAT) operates a 24-hour bus route in Laughlin, covering the business district and residential area. The fare for those 18 and over is $1.50, and 75¢ for ages 65 and older and 5 to 17.

Taxi—Laughlin and Bullhead City both have taxi service, but the Arizona-based taxi companies are not allowed to operate in Nevada unless called to take a passenger from Laughlin into the state of Arizona; they are not allowed to take passengers from one casino to another or from one location in Nevada to another.

The Laughlin taxi companies charge a base fare of $2.20 plus $1.70 for each mile; 35¢ per minute waiting time. In Bullhead City, the base fare is $1.50 plus $1.50 for each mile.

Laughlin
Desert	(702) 298-7575
Lucky	(702) 298-2299

Bullhead City
Bullhead City Taxi/Mojave	(928) 754-7433
Lucky	(928) 754-1100

Hospitals

Western Arizona Regional
  Medical Center
2735 Silver Creek Rd
Bullhead City, AZ
(928) 763-2273

UMC QuickCare
150 E Bruce Woodbury
Laughlin, NV
(702) 298-3364

AAA/California State Automobile Association

Office hours: Mon-Fri 8:30 am-5:30 pm

Henderson District Office
601 Whitney Ranch Dr, Ste A
Henderson, NV
(702) 458-2323

Las Vegas District Office
3312 W Charleston Blvd
Las Vegas, NV
(702) 870-9171

Summerlin District Office
8440 W Lake Mead Blvd, Ste 203
Las Vegas
(702) 360-3151

Visitor Services

Bullhead Area Chamber of
  Commerce
1251 Hwy 95
Bullhead City, AZ
(928) 754-4121
Office hours: Mon-Fri 8 am-5 pm

Laughlin Visitors Bureau
1555 Casino Dr
PO Box 502
Laughlin, NV 89029
(702) 298-3321, (800) 452-8445
Office hours: Daily 8 am-4:30 pm

OATMAN *23 miles SE of Bullhead City, Ariz via SR 95 and Boundary Cone Rd, on historic Route 66 (Oatman Hwy). (928) 768-6222.* Located in the rugged Black Mountains between Kingman and Bullhead City on historic Route 66, Oatman is an old mining town that has been seen in many movies and TV shows and is still brimming with the fervor of the Old West. Many of the original buildings are still in use, housing tourist-oriented enterprises, as well as a post office and several Western-style restaurants and saloons.

This once-prosperous gold-mining community flourished from 1905 to 1942, its local mines yielding nearly $36 million in gold at the peak of production. The onset of World War II led to the town's demise, when Congress halted all mining not essential to the war effort; mining activity resumed in recent years but ceased again in 1998 when the price of gold fell below a cost-productive level.

Today Oatman has about 150 residents, down from a whopping 10,000 during its heyday in the 1930s. Oatman's fortuitous position along the original Route 66 (US 66) from Chicago to Los Angeles has undoubtedly helped preserve it; this town was an important last stop for travelers before entering the Mojave Desert into California.

A number of Wild West-style attractions can be seen here, including the afternoon **gunfights** staged daily by the Ghostrider Gunfighters and their female counterparts, the Oatman Gold Diggers; shotgun weddings, with surprise interruptions by the aforementioned gunfighters; the Oatman Jail (now a museum); the historic Oatman Hotel, where movie legends Clark Gable and Carole Lombard spent their wedding night in 1939; and the town's unofficial welcoming committee of **wild burros**. These cute but stubborn animals are descendants of the burros miners turned loose years ago. They freely roam the streets in search of carrot handouts, a snack that can be purchased in local stores, but visitors are strongly discouraged from feeding them anything else.

The spectacular scenery offered up on the road through the Black Mountains, from Topock (on I-40) north to Oatman along Historic Route

Historic Route 66 offers spectacular mountain scenery near Oatman.

Staged gunfights erupt regularly on the streets of Oatman.

66 (Oatman Highway), may be the biggest attraction of all. For another **scenic drive** take Route 66 northeast out of Oatman to Kingman. The road goes past the historic mining camp of **Gold Road**, climbs to the summit of the Black Mountains, then crosses the wide Sacramento Valley to **Kingman**.

At times the road becomes a series of narrow hairpin curves as it winds its way up to the pass. But those with an adventurous spirit will be rewarded with panoramic views of Arizona and Nevada (maybe even California on a clear day) from the tri-state lookout point just before the summit of Sitgreaves Pass. From here, descend the eastern slope of the Black Mountains into the Sacramento Valley, an area populated with creosote bushes, yucca plants and, in season, a sprinkling of wildflowers. For the return to the Laughlin Bridge, take SR 68 west from Kingman across the flat Sacramento Valley, through a pass at the north end of the Black Mountains and down into the Colorado River Valley back to the

bridge. Total mileage (from Oatman) is 60 miles. **Note:** This trip is not recommended for large RVs or trailers.

Caution: When exploring near these areas, a four-wheel-drive vehicle is recommended for travel on unpaved roads. Flash flooding can occur during summer thunderstorms, and heavy rains are possible in any season. When exploring old gold camps, watch out for unfenced mine shafts and pits. Never enter abandoned mines; deep shafts, rotted timbers, and flammable or poisonous gases can be concealed in the tunnels.

Bartels' Stage Line *Oatman, Ariz. (928) 768-1600. $25 per person; ages 3-12, $12.50.* This one-hour narrated tour takes visitors through the ruins of the Gold Roads in an authentic replica of an 1880s stagecoach.

Gold Road Mine *On Historic Route 66, 2½ miles NE of Oatman, Ariz. (928) 768-1600. Open daily 10 am-5 pm. Basic tour (1 hr): adults $12, ages 4-11 $6; 3 and under, free. Extended tour (2½ hrs): $24.*

Extreme tour (4 hrs.): $50 (by reservation only; minimum age 13). Surface tour (I hr): $10. This mine, begun by a Mexican prospector who tripped over a chunk of quartz while searching for his lost burro, has been in production off and on for over 100 years. The tours start with a bumpy ride up a steep hill on a vehicle called a "getman," so named because it gets men up to and down from work. The basic tour takes visitors about 300 feet underground in a historic mine; a signpost marks a point where visitors are directly under Route 66. The extended and extreme tours explore other areas of the mine, while the surface tour focuses on gold ore processing.

RAMADA EXPRESS HOTEL & CASINO *In Laughlin at 2121 S Casino Dr. (800) 243-6846.*

American Heroes Foundation Museum *Open daily 8 am-5 pm. Free.* Thousands of personal mementos have been donated to this museum. Exhibits include diaries, medals, uniforms, military equipment, flags and models. There are also home-front items such as rationing stamps and propaganda pamphlets. The museum focuses on the WW II era, although there are small exhibits from the Korean and Vietnam wars.

Gambling Train of Laughlin *Open Mon-Thu 11 am-7 pm, Fri-Sun 10 am-10 pm. Free.* This narrow-gauge train offers rides (but no gambling) around this railroad-themed hotel. The locomotive is a replica of the Genoa, an 1890s-era steam engine that hauled freight and passengers on the Virginia and Truckee line in western Nevada.

RIVER WALK *Don Laughlin's Riverside Resort to River Palms Resort Casino. Open 24 hours daily. Free.* A stroll on this footpath along the river (accessed by walking through or between the hotels) provides a respite from the casinos and a pleasant way to experience the Colorado.

GUIDED TOURS

The tours listed in this section generally last less than a day. (More extensive touring information is available in the Las Vegas Valley chapter.) Be sure to contact the companies in advance for complete information. Scheduled tours are subject to cancellation if there is an insufficient number of passengers.

Tours listed are provided as a convenience for our readers; inclusion in this publication does not imply endorsement by the Automobile Club of Southern California.

LAUGHLIN RIVER TOURS, INC. *Laughlin. (702) 298-1047, (800) 228-9825. Depending on cruise, departures at Edgewater, Flamingo Laughlin or River Palms boat docks. Tickets available at docks of all 3 hotels.* Laughlin-Bullhead City area tours take place aboard a paddle-wheel boat.

U.S.S. RIVERSIDE *At Don Laughlin's Riverside Resort Hotel & Casino, 1650 S Casino Dr, Laughlin. (702) 298-2535, ext 5770, (800) 227-3849, ext 5770. Departures from Don Laughlin's Riverside boat dock. Ticket booth located on the ground level of the hotel, next to boat dock.* Boat tours of the Laughlin-Bullhead City area and Davis Dam. Weddings held aboard.

SHOWROOM ENTERTAINMENT

Laughlin does not offer the elaborate, long-running stage shows for which Las Vegas is famous. But its showrooms, cabarets and lounges do offer a variety of entertainment ranging from headline performers to lounge acts. While the facilities listed here seat 500 or more, many smaller venues are popular as well.

Showroom listing does not imply AAA endorsement for the lodging establishment. For the most current information, refer to the Auto Club's Las Vegas Shows schedule, available to AAA members at all Southern California district offices.

Lounge entertainment is available at all of the casinos, although some do not offer shows on Monday. The Riverside's Western Ballroom on the second floor of the hotel's south tower features a tea dance every Sunday from 2 to 6 p.m.; reservations are not required. In the evenings, the ballroom features live country music and dancing on its 1400-square-foot dance floor. Also, the Ramada Express offers dance contests Tuesday through Saturday at 4 p.m. in the Caboose Lounge. Times and prices vary with entertainers.

DON LAUGHLIN'S RIVERSIDE RESORT HOTEL & CASINO *1650 S Casino Dr. (702) 298-2535, ext 616, (800) 227-3849.*

Don's Celebrity Theatre—*Reservations recommended.* Top-name entertainment.

FLAMINGO LAUGHLIN *1900 S Casino Dr. (702) 298-5111, (800) 435-8469.*

Amphitheater—Outdoor seating in spring and fall. Top-name entertainment.

HARRAH'S CASINO HOTEL *2900 W Casino Dr. (702) 298-4600.*
Rio Vista Outdoor Amphitheater—Top name entertainment.

RAMADA EXPRESS HOTEL & CASINO *2121 S Casino Dr. (702) 298-4200; (800) 243-6846.*

Pavilion Theater—Top-name entertainment and *On the Wings of Eagles (Indefinitely). Daily 10 am-3 pm on the hour. Free.* A tribute to the men and women who served in our armed forces from World War II through Desert Storm is projected simultaneously on four movie screens.

RIVER PALMS RESORT CASINO *2700 S Casino Dr. (702) 298-2242, (800) 835-7904.*
Bermuda Club—Revues and top-name entertainment.

ANNUAL EVENTS

Car and motorcycle rallies, rodeos, fireworks displays and even a sidewalk egg fry are among the many community events that Laughlin and environs offer annually. For information about each event, please call the telephone numbers shown, or consult with the local chamber of commerce or visitor information bureau.

In addition, casino tournaments take place in many Laughlin casinos. Anyone interested in these tournaments should contact the hotel or venue directly for dates and play information; room reservations should be made well in advance, as room space is often at a premium during a tournament.

January

BED RACES AND CHAMBER POT PARADE *Oatman, Ariz. (928) 768-6222.* Five-person teams push old iron beds to the finish line on a zigzag race course. Costumed race contestants parade down the street, competing for best-costume prizes.

LAUGHLIN DESERT CHALLENGE *Starts and finishes at corner of Big Bend Dr and Edison Wy, Laughlin. (800) 227-5245.* More than 200 of the world's top drivers compete over two days in an off-road race through the rough terrain outside of Laughlin.

TURQUOISE CIRCUIT FINALS RODEO *Corner of Marina Blvd and Hwy 95, Bullhead City, Ariz. (928) 754-4121.* This PRCA-sanctioned event features three days of calf-roping, bareback bull- and bronco-riding, music, food and vendor booths.

displays of rocks, including rocks for purchase, and demonstrations of lapidary, jewelry, minerals, faceting and a silent auction.

CLARK GABLE-CAROLE LOMBARD LOOK-ALIKE CONTEST *Oatman Hotel, Oatman, Ariz. (928) 768-4274.* Individuals are given the opportunity to exchange vows, and even spend the night, in the same bridal suite where Clark Gable and Carole Lombard spent their honeymoon.

LAUGHLIN RODEO DAYS *Casino Dr, Laughlin. (702) 298-2214, (800) 227-5245.* This five-day PRCA Rodeo featuring the Laughlin River Stampede draws more than 500 participants, who compete for prize money in eight traditional rodeo events. Entertainment, vendor booths, country-western dances and festivities are part of the fun, and take place at area resorts and hotels.

March

SILVERY COLORADO GEM AND MINERAL SHOW *Bullhead City Jr High School, Bullhead City, Ariz. (928) 763-8271.* This two-day event features

April

DESERT TWIRLERS DO IT ON THE RIVER JAMBOREE *Mohave Jr. High School, Bullhead City, Ariz. (928) 763-3424.* This two-day event features square and round dancing, plus daytime workshops.

LAUGHLIN RIVER RUN *Casino Dr, Laughlin. (702) 298-2212, (800) 227-5245.* This four-day motorcycle rally features Harley-Davidsons and is billed as the West Coast's largest motorcycle event. Vendor booths sport a wide range of merchandise, such as motorcycle accessories, silver and turquoise jewelry, and leather apparel. Live entertainment and food are also featured.

June

RIVER DAYS *Colorado Riverfront, Laughlin. (702) 298-2214, (800) 227-5245.* Amateur and professional riders compete over three days in Formula One races on the Colorado River along the Laughlin shoreline. An exposition showcases the latest in personal watercraft equipment and accessories.

July

FOURTH OF JULY FESTIVITIES *Various locations. (702) 298-2214 (Laughlin); (928) 565-2204 (Bullhead City, Ariz.), (928) 768-6222 (Oatman, Ariz.).* Independence Day is celebrated in a wide range of community events.

OATMAN SIDEWALK EGG FRY *Oatman, Ariz. (928) 768-6222.* This annual Fourth of July event features an egg-and-spoon race, traditional sidewalk egg fry, egg-toss and chicken-leg contest, and usually a gun-fighter reunion.

September

OATMAN GOLD CAMP DAYS *Oatman, Ariz. (928) 768-6222.* The internationally famous Burro Biscuit Throwing Contest is the highlight of this Labor Day weekend event. Other activities include a crazy hat contest, chili cookoff and barbecue.

RODDIN' ON THE RIVER *Don Laughlin's Riverside Resort Hotel & Casino, Laughlin. (928) 768-2197.* Hot rods, classic customs and mini trucks are showcased during this four-day event. Highlights include slow drags and valve-cover races, and competitions for prizes.

November

CHRISTMAS BUSH CONTEST *Oatman, Ariz. (928) 768-6222.* Shopkeepers and residents decorate bushes for the holidays, beginning in November, along Historic Route 66 leading into Oatman from the west.

December

PARADE OF LIGHTS *Katherine's Landing, Ariz. (928) 754-3245.* Boats gather on Lake Mohave to celebrate the Christmas season with an evening's blaze of festive, twinkling lights.

NEW YEAR'S EVE CELEBRATIONS *(702) 298-2214 (Laughlin).* Traditional New Year's Eve festivities take place on both sides of the Colorado River.

Recreation

With an average of nearly 300 sunny days a year, Las Vegas and the Laughlin-Bullhead City areas are ideal spots for outdoor sports. Not only are there acres of lush green golf courses, tennis courts and seemingly endless swimming pools, but the canyons and mountains offer horseback riding amid dramatic backdrops, and the Lake Mead National Recreation Area provides year-round boating, fishing, water-skiing and more.

Golfing

Golf is one of the principal outdoor attractions in Las Vegas, as well as a popular sport in Laughlin-Bullhead City. Las Vegas features several championship courses, some of which host PGA and LPGA tournaments, plus several less demanding courses where the weekend golfer can enjoy a quick round. The desert climate offers nearly ideal playing conditions all year, with the exception of very high midday temperatures in July and August. In summer, golfers should arrange an early starting time to avoid the extreme heat.

Public, semi-private and private courses are listed alphabetically by city. Information given for each course includes its name, location, street address, phone number, yardage, par, slope, USGA ratings (from the preferred tee of the course), greens fees and facilities. Greens fees are given for weekday and weekend play during peak season. Some courses may not allow walking so the greens fee includes the mandatory golf cart fee. Some courses have senior citizen rates; call for information. Unless otherwise stated, each course is open daily.

Military golf courses listed in this publication include a phone number; call for information about play. Nine-hole courses may show par, slope and USGA rating that reflect nine holes played twice. It follows that a 9-hole course may list an 18-hole fee because they require 18 holes of play.

All semi-private and private courses have restrictions on public play ranging from members and guests only to liberal reciprocal agreements with members of other courses. Information on private courses is not listed, but a telephone number is provided for obtaining information about reciprocal play. As it is impossible to list all of the restrictions for each course, telephoning the course is highly recommended in lieu of knowing a member. Reservations are advised at most courses; some country clubs require reservations months in advance.

Information in this section is published as it is received from the individual courses. The listings have been made as complete as possible.

Boulder City

BOULDER CITY GOLF COURSE
Public
SE of US 93 off Buchanan Blvd; 1 Clubhouse Dr. (702) 293-9236. Daily rate: walking, $27; cart, $36. The course is 18

holes; 6132 yards; par 72; 103 slope; 68.3 rating. Clubhouse, golf shop, professional, power carts, rental clubs, driving range; coffee shop, snack bar.

Henderson

ANTHEM COUNTRY CLUB Private *(702) 614-5050.*

BLACK MOUNTAIN GOLF AND COUNTRY CLUB Semi-Private
½ mile SW of US 93 (Boulder Hwy); 500 Greenway Rd. (702) 565-7933. Closed Dec 25. Rates including golf cart: Mon-Thu $80, Fri-Sun $90. The course is 18 holes; 6550 yards; par 72; 123 slope; 71.2 rating. Clubhouse, locker room, golf shop, professional, power carts, rental clubs, driving range; restaurant, coffee shop, snack bar.

DESERT WILLOW GOLF COURSE Public
1½ mi S of I-215 off Green Valley Pkwy; 2020 Horizon Ridge. (702) 263-4653. Rate including mandatory golf cart: Mon-Thu $50, Fri-Sun $60. The course is 18 holes; 3800 yards; par 60; 91 slope; 59.1 rating. Clubhouse, golf shop, professional, power carts, rental clubs, driving range; restaurant, snack bar.

DRAGON RIDGE GOLF CLUB Private
(702) 614-4444.

THE LEGACY GOLF CLUB Public
N of SR 146 (Lake Mead Dr) off N Green Valley Pkwy; 130 Par Excellence Dr. (702) 897-2187. Closed Dec 25. Rate including mandatory golf cart: Mon-Thu $130, Fri-Sun $145; twilight, $80. The course is 18

holes; 6211 yards; par 72; 118 slope; 69.1 rating. Clubhouse, golf shop, professional, power carts, rental clubs, driving range; restaurant, snack bar.

REVERE AT ANTHEM GOLF CLUB Public
10 mi S of I-215 via Eastern Av, Anthem; 2600 Evergreen Oaks Dr. (702) 259-4653. Daily rate: $75-205. The course is 18 holes; 5941 yards; par 72; 125 slope; 68.2 rating. Clubhouse, golf shop, professional, power carts, rental clubs, driving range; snack bar.

Golf is a popular pastime at Las Vegas' numerous courses.

RIO SECO GOLF CLUB Private
(702) 867-3226.

SOUTHSHORE GOLF CLUB AT LAKE LAS VEGAS Private
(702) 558-0022.

WILDHORSE GOLF CLUB Public
3 mi W of US 95 via Sunset Rd and Green Valley Pkwy; 2100 W Warm Springs Rd. (702) 434-9009. Daily rates including mandatory golf cart: $25-180. The course is 18 holes; 5900 yards; par 72; 121 slope; 69.5 rating. Golf shop, professional, power carts, rental clubs, driving range; restaurant, snack bar.

Las Vegas

ANGEL PARK GOLF CLUB Public
3 mi W of SR 95 off Summerlin Pkwy; 100 S Rampart Blvd. (702) 254-4653. Closed Dec 25. Daily rates including mandatory golf cart: $20-140. The **Mountain Course** is 18 holes; 5718 yards; par 71; 116 slope; 67.8 rating. The **Palm Course** is 18 holes; 5438 yards; par 70; 113 slope; 67.8 rating. The **Cloud 9 Course** is 9 holes; 1341 yards; par 27. Clubhouse, locker room, golf shop, professional, power carts, rental clubs, driving range, night lighting for short course and driving range; restaurant, snack bar.

BADLANDS GOLF CLUB Public
3½ mi W of US 95 via Summerlin Pkwy off Rampart Blvd; 9119 Alta Dr. (702) 363-0754. Rates including mandatory golf cart: Mon-Thu $90, Fri-Sun $100. The **Desperado/Diablo Course** is 18 holes; 6430 yards; par 72; 113 slope; 67.8 rating. The **Diablo/Outlaw Course** is 18 holes; 6430 yards; par 72; 116 slope; 68.2 rating. The **Desperado/Outlaw Course** is 18 holes; 6175 yards; par 72; 116 slope; 67.6 rating. Clubhouse, driving range, golf shop, professional, power carts, rental clubs; restaurant.

BALI HAI GOLF CLUB Private
(888) 397-2499.

CALLAWAY GOLF CENTER Private
(702) 896-4100.

CANYON GATE COUNTRY CLUB Private
(702) 363-0303.

CRAIG RANCH GOLF COURSE Public
3 mi N off I-15/US 93; 628 W Craig Rd. (702) 642-9700. Daily rate: walking $17; cart $25. The course is 18 holes; 6001 yards; par 70; 105 slope; 66.8 rating.

Clubhouse, golf shop, professional, power carts, rental clubs, driving range; snack bar.

DESERT PINES GOLF CLUB Public
Just N of US 95 via Eastern Ave; 3415 E Bonanza Rd. (702) 388-4400; reservations (888) 397-2499. Rates including mandatory golf cart: Mon-Thu $140, Fri-Sun $190. The course is 18 holes; 6810 yards; par 71; 122 slope; 70.4 rating. Clubhouse, golf shop, professional, power carts, rental clubs, driving range, night lighting for driving range; cocktail lounge, restaurant, snack bar.

DESERT ROSE GOLF COURSE Public
6 mi E of I-15 off Sahara Ave; 5483 Clubhouse Dr. (702) 431-4653. Daily rate: Mon-Thu $70; Fri-Sun $80. The course is 18 holes; 6511 yards; par 71; 117 slope; 69.6 rating. Clubhouse, golf shop, professional, power carts, rental clubs, driving range; restaurant, snack bar.

EAGLE CREST GOLF COURSE Private
(702) 240-1320.

HIGHLAND FALLS GOLF COURSE Semi-Private
10 mi NW of downtown off Lake Mead Blvd; 10201 Sun City Blvd. (702) 254-7010. Daily rate including mandatory golf cart: $65-105. The course is 18 holes; 6512 yards; par 72; 127 slope; 72.3 rating. Clubhouse, golf shop, professional, power carts, rental clubs, driving range; coffee shop, restaurant, snack bar.

LAS VEGAS COUNTRY CLUB Private
(702) 734-1132.

LAS VEGAS GOLF CLUB Public
1½ mi N of US 95 via Decatur Blvd; 4300 Washington Ave. (702) 646-3003. Daily

rate: Mon-Thu $69; Fri-Sun $89. The course is 18 holes; 5918 yards; par 72; 105 slope; 6801 rating. Golf shop, professional, power carts, rental clubs, driving range, night lighting for driving range; snack bar.

LAS VEGAS NATIONAL GOLF CLUB Public

3 mi E of I-15 via Flamingo Rd and Maryland Pkwy; 1911 E Desert Inn Rd. (702) 734-1796. Daily rates including mandatory golf cart: $50-200. The course is 18 holes; 6418 yards; par 71; 121 slope; 70.2 rating. Clubhouse, locker room, golf shop, professional, power carts, rental clubs, driving range, night lighting for driving range; restaurant, snack bar.

LAS VEGAS PAIUTE RESORT Public

18 mi NW of downtown off US 95, exit 95 (Snow Mountain), 1½ mi E to 10325 Nu-Wav Kaiv Blvd. (702) 658-1400. Two courses; rates for both including mandatory golf cart: Mon-Thu $140; Fri-Sun $155. The **Snow Mountain Course** is 18 holes; 6035 yards; par 72; 116 slope; 68.6 rating. The **Sun Mountain Course** is 18 holes; 6074 yards; par 72; 116 slope; 68.6 rating. Clubhouse, golf shop, professional, power carts, rental clubs, driving range; banquet facilities, restaurant, snack bar.

LOS PRADOS GOLF COURSE Public

On Lone Mountain Rd and Los Prados Blvd; 5150 Los Prados Cir. (702) 645-5696. Closed Dec 25. Rates: Mon-Thu $40, Fri-Sun and holidays $50. The course is 18 holes; 4937 yards; par 70; 101 slope; 63.4 rating. Clubhouse, locker room, golf shop, professional, power carts, rental clubs; restaurant, coffee shop, snack bar.

NORTH LAS VEGAS COMMUNITY 3 PAR GOLF COURSE Public

1 mi W of I-15 off Cheyenne Ave; 324 E Brooks Ave. (702) 633-1833. Rates: Mon-Fri $7.50, Sat-Sun and holidays $8.50; weekday, senior and student discounts. The course is 9 holes; 1128 yards; par 70; N/A slope; N/A rating. Clubhouse, rental clubs, driving range, night lighting; coffee shop, snack bar.

PAINTED DESERT GOLF COURSE Public

¼ mi W of US 95 (Tonopah Hwy) off Ann Rd; 5555 Painted Mirage Wy. (702) 645-2568; 645-2570. Rates including mandatory golf cart: Mon-Thu $125, Fri-Sun $165. The course is 18 holes; 6323 yards; par 72; 128 slope; 71.0 rating. Clubhouse, golf shop, professional, power carts, rental clubs, driving range; restaurant, snack bar.

PALM VALLEY GOLF CLUB Semi-Private

10 mi NW of downtown off Lake Mead Blvd; 9201-B Del Webb Blvd. (702) 363-4373. Daily rate including mandatory golf cart: $50-110. The course is 18 holes; 6341 yards; par 72; 124 slope; 69.8 rating. Clubhouse, golf shop, professional, power carts, rental clubs, driving range; restaurant, snack bar.

RED ROCK COUNTRY CLUB Private

(702) 360-5959.

REFLECTION BAY GOLF CLUB Public

8 mi E of I-515 off SR 146 via Lake Las Vegas Pkwy; 75 Monte Lago Bl. (702) 470-4653. Daily rate including mandatory golf cart: $235. The course is 18 holes; 6391 yards; par 72; 128 slope; 70.3 rating. Clubhouse, locker room, golf shop, professional, power carts, rental clubs, driving range; restaurant, snack bar.

RHODES RANCH GOLF CLUB
Private
(702) 740-4114.

THE ROYAL LINKS Public
6 mi E of Las Vegas Bl on Flamingo Bl;
5995 E Vegas Valley Dr. (702) 450-8123.
Daily rate including mandatory golf cart:
Mon-Thu $225, Fri-Sun $275. The course
is 18 holes; 5142 yards; par 72; 135
slope; 73.5 rating. Clubhouse, locker
room, golf shop, professional, power
carts, rental clubs, driving range;
restaurant, snack bar.

SIENA GOLF CLUB Public
10 mi W of I-15 off Sahara Ave W and
Town Center Dr; 10575 Siena Monte Ave.
(702) 341-9200. Daily rate including
mandatory golf cart: Mon-Thu $70-130,
Fri-Sun $90-160. The course is 18 holes;
5613 yards; par 72; 115 slope; 66.3 rating. Golf shop, professional, power
carts, rental clubs, driving range;
restaurant, snack bar.

SILVERSTONE GOLF CLUB Private
(877) 888-2127.

SOUTHERN HIGHLANDS GOLF
CLUB Private
(702) 263-1000.

SPANISH TRAIL GOLF AND
COUNTRY CLUB Private
(702) 364-0357.

STALLION MOUNTAIN COUN-
TRY CLUB Private
(702) 4506-8000.

SUNRISE VISTA GOLF COURSE
Military
(702) 652-2602.

TOURNAMENT PLAYERS CLUB
AT THE CANYONS Public
4 mi W of US 95 off Summerlin Pkwy,
Town Center and Canyon Run drs; 9851
Canyon Run Dr. (702) 256-2000. Rates
including mandatory golf cart: Mon-Thu

$175, Fri-Sun $230. The course is 18
holes; 6110 yards; par 71; 118 slope;
67.7 rating. Clubhouse, locker room,
golf shop, professional, power carts,
rental clubs, driving range; restaurant,
snack bar.

Laughlin-Bullhead City

CHAPARRAL COUNTRY CLUB
Public
7 mi S of Laughlin Bridge via SR 95; 1260
Mohave Dr, Bullhead City, Ariz. (928)
758-3939. Closed Dec 25. Daily rates
including mandatory golf cart: $20-30.
The course is 18 holes; 4626 yards; par
64; 100 slope; 62.1 rating. Clubhouse,
golf shop, professional, power carts,
rental clubs; restaurant, snack bar.

DESERT LAKES GOLF COURSE
Public
13 mi S of Laughlin Bridge via SR 95, east on
Joy Ln; 5835 Desert Lakes Dr, Bullhead City,
Ariz. (928) 768-1000. Daily rates including
mandatory golf cart: $41-81; call for sum-
mer, senior and twilight rates. The course is
18 holes; 6267 yards; par 72; 115 slope;
69.1 rating. Clubhouse, golf shop, professional, power carts, rental clubs, driving range; restaurant, snack bar.

EMERALD RIVER GOLF COURSE
Public
1½ mi E of Needles Hwy; 1155 S Casino
Dr, Laughlin. (702) 298-0061. Rates
including mandatory golf cart: Mon-Thu
$45-80; Fri-Sun $45-95. The course is 18
holes; 6050 yards; par 72; 131 slope;
69.1 rating. Clubhouse, coffee shop,
golf shop, professional, power carts,
rental clubs, driving range; snack bar.

MOJAVE RESORT GOLF CLUB
Public
9 mi S of Laughlin off Needles Hwy; 9905
Aha Macav Pkwy, Laughlin. (702) 535-
4653. Rates including mandatory golf cart:

Mon-Thu $65; Fri-Sun $75. The course is 18 holes; 5959 yards; par 72; 115 slope; 68.5 rating. Clubhouse, locker room, golf shop, professional, power carts, rental clubs, driving range; coffee shop, snack bar.

RIVERVIEW GOLF COURSE Public
5 mi S of Laughlin Bridge via SR 95, E to 2000 E Ramar Rd, Bullhead City, Ariz. (928) 763-1818. Daily rate: $15. The course is 9 holes; 1160 yards; par 27; N/A rating. Clubhouse, golf shop, professional, hand carts, hand carts, power carts, rental clubs.

Primm

PRIMM VALLEY GOLF CLUB
Public
35 mi S of Las Vegas at 1 Yates Rd. (702) 679-5510. Daily rate including mandatory golf cart: Mon-Thu $150; Fri-Sun $195. The **Lakes Course** is 18 holes; 6444 yards; par 71; 126 slope; 71.5 rating. The **Desert Course** is 18 holes; 6540 yards; par 72; 130 slope; 71.7 rating. Clubhouse, golf shop, professional, power carts, rental clubs, driving range; cocktail lounge.

Horseback Riding

Las Vegas

COWBOY TRAIL RIDES, INC. *800 N Rainbow, Ste 204. (702) 387-2457. Open daily. Guided rides ranging from 1 hour to overnight; prices $45 and up, depending on length of ride. Reservations recommended.* Riders traverse scenic Red Rock Canyon and Mt. Charleston on trips that contain mustang viewing, rim rides, twilight barbecues as well as a combo helicopter ride package.

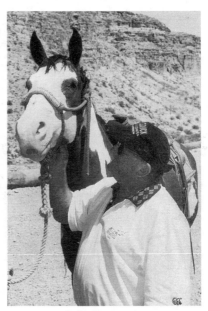

Outdoor activities include horsing around with a new friend at Red Rock Canyon.

Red Rock Canyon National Conservation Area

BONNIE SPRINGS OLD NEVADA
Off SR 159/W Charleston Blvd, 5½ mi S of Red Rock Canyon Visitor Center; 1 Gun Fighter Ln. (702) 875-4191. Open daily; first ride departs at 9 am, last at 3:15 pm, Jun through Sep at 5:45 pm. $25 per person; children age 5 and under not admitted. No reservations. One-hour guided rides traverse scenic Red Rock Canyon.

Spring Mountains National Recreation Area

SAGE BRUSH RANCH *12000 W Ann Rd. (702) 655-7991. Open daily. $25-129. Reservations required.* Rides may include breakfast, lunch or dinner.

The desert climate offers nearly ideal playing conditions year round.

Rock Climbing

Red Rock Canyon National Conservation Area

SKY'S THE LIMIT *(702) 363-4533, (800) 733-7597. Half-day rock-climbing lessons, $189. Reservations recommended.* Participants learn climbing and rappelling fundamentals from experienced instructors amid the scenery of Red Rock Canyon. Climbing shoes and equipment are provided. Day hikes also available.

Tennis & Racquetball

Tennis and racquetball enthusiasts will find plenty of places to hone their skills in Las Vegas. A number of publicly maintained parks have courts, as do many of the resort hotels and private clubs. Most of the courts are lighted for nighttime play. The hotels that allow visitors to use their facili-

ties often give priority to their registered guests, restricting others to open courts. Hotels whose courts are restricted to guests only are not listed here. It is always a good idea to phone ahead, since hours and regulations governing play are subject to change.

Public courts operate on a first-come, first-served basis and are open daily, generally from 6 a.m. to 11 p.m. For information about public courts, call (702) 455-8200.

Las Vegas

BALLY'S LAS VEGAS Semi-Private *3645 Las Vegas Blvd S. (702) 967-4598. Open daily, 7 am-7 pm. Hotel guests, $10 per hour; nonguests, $15 per hour. Reservations required for play between 8:30 am and 5:30 pm. 8 lighted outdoor tennis courts.*

FLAMINGO LAS VEGAS Semi-Private *3555 Las Vegas Blvd S. (702) 733-3444.*

Open daily, 7 am; Mon-Thu to 7 pm; closing hour varies on weekends. $12 per hour for hotel guests, $20 for nonguests. Reservations required. 4 lighted tennis courts.

HIDDEN PALMS PARK Public
8855 Hidden Palms Pkwy. 2 lighted tennis courts.

LAS VEGAS ATHLETIC CLUB-MARYLAND PARKWAY Semi-Private
2655 S Maryland Pkwy. (702) 734-5822. Open 24 hours. Guest pass, $15. Reservations available. 5 racquetball courts, 25-meter lap pool.

LAS VEGAS ATHLETIC CLUB-WEST SAHARA Semi-Private
5200 W Sahara Ave. (702) 364-5822. Open daily; Mon-Fri 5 am-midnight, Sat-Sun 7 am-10 pm. Guest pass $15. Reservations available. 2 racquetball courts, 25-meter lap pool.

LAS VEGAS SPORTING HOUSE Semi-Private
3025 Industrial Rd. (702) 733-8999. Open 24 hours. $15 per person, includes all facilities. 10 racquetball courts; 2 squash courts; 2 lighted tennis courts.

LAURELWOOD PARK Public
4300 Newcastle Rd. 2 lighted tennis courts.

MONTE CARLO RESORT & CASINO Semi-Private
3770 Las Vegas Blvd S. (702) 730-7411. Open daily, 7 am-11 pm. Hotel guests $12, nonguests $18. Reservations required. 3 lighted tennis courts.

PARADISE PARK COMMUNITY CENTER Public
4770 S Harrison Dr. 2 lighted tennis courts.

PAUL MEYER PARK Public
4525 New Forest Dr. 2 lighted tennis courts.

SUNRISE PARK AND COMMUNITY CENTER Public
2240 Linn Ln. 2 lighted tennis courts.

SUNSET PARK Public
2601 E Sunset Rd. (702) 260-9803. 8 lighted tennis courts.

UNIVERSITY OF NEVADA, LAS VEGAS Semi-Private
McDermott Complex, on campus near Harmon Ave and Swenson St. Tennis reservations (702) 895-4489; racquetball reservations (702) 895-3150. Tennis courts

♠ Spa Facilities

After a long day of exploring the diverse offerings of Las Vegas, your tired and aching muscles may be screaming out for a relaxing massage, facial or an herbal wrap. On the other hand, maybe your body is used to a regular workout and you feel guilty about lounging around the hotel pool or casino all day, or worse, the number of buffets you've been frequenting. Alas, help is readily available. Many of the large resort hotels feature complete spa facilities, including whirlpool, sauna, massage, exercise programs (aquatic, aerobic), gym equipment, and more. Hotel spa and health club privileges often carry a fee; policies vary at each establishment. Some health clubs in hotels admit only registered guests. Public health clubs are numerous in the city, and most of the larger ones offer daily passes; check the local telephone directory yellow pages under "Health Clubs" for further information.

open daily 8 am-10 pm. Guest fee $5. Racquetball courts open daily; Mon-Fri 6 am-10 pm, Sat 8 am-6 pm, Sun 10 am-6 pm. Guest fee, $4. Reservations advised. 12 lighted tennis courts; 8 indoor racquetball courts.

WHITNEY PARK AND COMMUNITY CENTER Public
5700 E Missouri Ave. 3 lighted tennis courts.

WINCHESTER PARK AND COMMUNITY CENTER Public
3130 S McLeod Dr. 2 lighted tennis courts.

WINTERWOOD PARK Public
5310 Consul Ave. 2 lighted tennis courts.

Laughlin

MOUNTAIN VIEW PARK Public
Needles Hwy, S of Desert Rd. 2 lighted tennis courts.

Water Recreation

Entries for this section are listed north to south in three regions along the Colorado River: Lake Mead, Lake Mohave and Below Davis Dam. The first two fall within the Lake Mead National Recreation Area, which stretches from the upper reaches of Lake Mead to Davis Dam at the southern tip of Lake Mohave. The river below Davis Dam includes the Laughlin/Bullhead City area and southward toward Needles, California.

Lake Mead

25 mi SE of Las Vegas; 4 mi NE of Boulder City. Information available through the

Lake Mead National Recreation Area features a variety of water sports.

Lake Mead National Recreation Area at either the Alan Bible Visitor Center on US 93, phone (702) 293-8990 or (702) 293-8906, or at any park ranger station. Elevation 1200. This 110-mile-long lake on the Colorado River extends from Hoover Dam to the Grand Canyon. The shoreline offers sandy beaches and sheltered coves, while the rugged desert terrain invites hiking and climbing. Lake activities encompass boating, swimming, sailing, water-skiing, scuba diving, sailboarding, use of personal watercraft and fishing. Complete recreation facilities are available at six sites operated by concessionaires of the National Park Service. Boaters should beware of sudden winds, floating debris, and underwater rocks and shoals caused by fluctuating water levels.

Boating

CALLVILLE BAY RESORT AND MARINA *22 mi NE of Henderson on SR 167, 4 mi S of Northshore Rd. (702) 565-*

8958. *Open daily.* Paved launch ramp, temporary mooring, slips, dry storage, auto/boat fuel, engine repairs, marine waste station. Rentals: Houseboats, motorboats (15 to 250 hp), fishing boats, personal watercraft. Marine hardware, campground, picnic area.

ECHO BAY RESORT AND MARINA *30 mi S of Overton off Northshore Rd.* (702) 394-4066. *Open daily.* Paved launch ramp, temporary mooring, slips, dry storage, auto/boat fuel, engine and hull repairs, marine waste station. Rentals: Houseboats, motorboats (15 to 150 hp), fishing tackle, water-skis, personal watercraft. Marine hardware, bait, groceries, ice, snack bar, restaurant, lodging, campground with hookups, picnic area.

HEMENWAY LAUNCH RAMP *5 mi NE of Boulder City off Lakeshore Rd; Lake Mead NRA.* (702) 293-8990. *Open daily.* Paved launch ramp. Wheelchair-accessible fishing dock nearby.

LAKE MEAD RESORT AND MARINA *7 mi NE of Boulder City; 322 Lakeshore Rd.* (702) 293-3484. *Open daily.* Paved launch ramp, slips, temporary mooring, dry storage, boat fuel. Rentals: Motorboats (140 hp). Lodging, public campgrounds, restaurant, store; picnic area nearby.

LAS VEGAS BAY MARINA *8 mi NE of Henderson off Lakeshore Rd.* (702) 565-9111. *Open daily.* Paved launch ramp, temporary mooring, slips, dry storage, auto/boat fuel, engine and hull repairs, marine waste station. Rentals: Motorboats (15 to 185 hp), water-skis, Waverunners. Marine hardware, bait, groceries, ice, restaurant, picnic area.

OVERTON BEACH RESORT AND MARINA *11 mi SE of Overton off Lakeshore Rd.* (702) 394-4040. *Open daily. Closed Dec. 25.* Paved launch ramp, temporary mooring, slips, dry storage, auto/boat fuel, engine and hull repairs, marine waste station. Rentals: Fishing boat (50 hp), patio boat, personal watercraft. Marine hardware, bait, groceries, ice, snack bar, RV sites with hookups.

TEMPLE BAR RESORT AND MARINA *28 mi NE of US 93 at the end of Temple Bar Rd.* (928) 767-3211. *Open daily. Closed Dec. 25.* Paved launch ramp, mooring, slips, dry storage, auto/boat fuel, engine/hull repairs, marine waste station. Rentals: Motorboats (15 to 150 hp), water-skis, personal watercraft. Cocktail lounge, marine hardware, bait, groceries, ice, restaurant, lodging, public campground, picnic area.

Fishing

Lake Mead offers some of the country's best fishing. Unlike some lakes, Lake

---

♠ More on the River

Visitors will find the Auto Club's *Explore! Colorado River Guide Map* a useful recreation map. The guide provides detailed map coverage and information on local activities, attractions, events and facilities. Members can obtain this publication at all Auto Club district offices in California and Nevada. Nonmembers should check with a local bookseller in Central or Southern California.

The beach at Harrah's Laughlin is a pleasant spot for taking a dip and enjoying the sight of passing riverboats.

Mead (and nearby Lake Mohave) has an open season on all species of fish year round. Largemouth bass, striped bass, channel catfish, black crappie and bluegill are popular catches; rangers or marina personnel can help point out the best fishing areas. Striped bass are most popular; some have tipped the scales at 50 pounds or more. A wheelchair-accessible fishing dock is located at Hemenway Fishing Point on Boulder Beach.

Swimming

Clear and clean water ideal for swimming, snorkeling and diving can be found at Lake Mead. The best seasons are spring, summer and fall, when water temperatures average about 78 degrees. Boulder Beach is a designated swimming area. Swim with caution and with a buddy, as no lifeguard services are provided. The scuba diving trail at north Boulder Beach provides a protected dive area.

Water-Skiing

The lake's wide basins offer perfect conditions for water-skiing. The sport is allowed on most of Lake Mead, except in the side canyons and for a few hundred feet north of Hoover Dam.

Lake Mohave

Accessible via US 95 and US 93. Information available through the Lake Mead National Recreation Area at either the Alan Bible Visitor Center (near Lake Mead on US 93), phone (702) 293-8990 or (702) 293-8906, or at any park ranger station. Elevation 675. This narrow lake, which stretches for 67 miles below Hoover Dam to Davis Dam, is lined by rock canyon walls, and has numerous coves and sandy beaches. Activities include boating, swimming, water-skiing, skin diving, sailboarding, use of personal watercraft and fishing. Boating facilities are located at three points along the lake. Boaters should beware of sudden winds and flash floods.

Boating

COTTONWOOD COVE RESORT AND MARINA *14 mi E of Searchlight at the end of Cottonwood Cove Rd. (702) 297-1464. Open daily.* Paved launch ramp, slips, dry storage, auto/boat fuel, engine repairs, temporary mooring, marine waste station. Rentals: Houseboats, motorboats (25 to 150 hp), personal watercraft, water-skis. Bait, groceries, ice, clothing, restaurant, lodging, RV sites with hookups, picnic and swimming areas.

LAKE MOHAVE RESORT AND MARINA *At Katherine Landing, 6 mi N of Bullhead City via Ariz SR 68 and Katherine Landing Rd, Bullhead City, Ariz. (928) 754-3245. Open daily.* Paved launch ramp, slips, temporary mooring, dry storage, boat fuel, engine repairs, marine waste station. Rentals: Houseboats, motorboats (15 to 150 hp), fishing tackle, water-skis, personal watercraft, houseboats. Marine hardware, bait, groceries, ice, snack bar, restaurant, lodging, RV sites with hookups, picnic area. Wheelchair-accessible fishing dock nearby.

PRINCESS COVE LAUNCH RAMP *Follow a graded dirt road 5 mi N of Katherine Landing, Bullhead City, Ariz. (928) 754-3272.* Paved launch ramp.

WILLOW BEACH HARBOR *14 mi S of Hoover Dam via US 93 and Willow Beach Rd; Willow Beach, Ariz. (928) 767-4747. Open daily. Closed Dec 25.* Paved launch ramp, slips, boat fuel. Rentals: Motorboats (25 to 150 hp), personal watercraft. Bait, groceries, ice, picnic area.

Fishing

Noted for its rainbow trout and bass fishing, Lake Mohave offers an open season on all species of fish year round. Trout spend the summer north of Willow Beach and migrate south from October through January; a fish hatchery at Willow Beach provides trout for planting in the lake. Rainbow trout are popular in the cold waters of upper Lake Mohave from Hoover Dam to Willow Beach, but the record sizes of the past have diminished to an occasional five pounds. Large-mouth bass prefer the deep water at the south end of the lake and

♠ Fishing Licenses

Anglers fishing from Arizona, California and Nevada must possess valid fishing licenses from the state concerned. In Arizona, persons 13 and under do not require a license, while in California persons 15 and under do not require one. In Nevada, a junior permit is required for anglers 12 to 15 years old. The rules and regulations of each state must be strictly adhered to, including within the Lake Mead National Recreation Area. Fishing on the Colorado River or Lake Mead requires a "special use" stamp affixed to a state-fishing license. An additional stamp is required for trout fishing. Fishing from shore on an Indian reservation requires a special fishing permit. Licenses and further information are available from the marinas or at local bait and tackle shops.

only move into shallow water to spawn; the best catches are taken from October to May. Trolling live bait at depths of 10 to 30 feet works well to lure them; fishing the coves with floating minnow-shaped lures is also effective during midday. Striped bass have become an increasingly common catch throughout much of the lake in recent years. July and August are the best months for finding catfish in the lake's small coves and inlets. February through April is crappie season; they can be found along the lower half of the lake. Mini-jigs, worms and minnows are the ticket for catching them. A wheelchair-accessible fishing dock is located at Katherine Landing. **Note:** There is a multiagency effort under way to protect endangered species of the Colorado River. Fishermen should identify and immediately release humpback chubs, bonytail chubs, razorback suckers and Colorado squawfish that they hook. Anglers who are unfamiliar with these species will find descriptions in the California and Arizona fishing regulations booklets that are available where licenses are sold.

Rainbow trout are popular in the cold waters of upper Lake Mohave from Hoover Dam to Willow Beach, but the record sizes of the past have diminished to an occasional five pounds. Large-mouth bass prefer the deep water at the south end of the lake and only move into shallow water to spawn; the best catches are taken from October to May. Trolling live bait at depths of 10 to 30 feet works well to lure them; fishing the coves with floating minnow-shaped lures is also effective during midday. Striped bass have become an increasingly common catch throughout much of

the lake in recent years. July and August are the best months for finding catfish in the lake's small coves and inlets. February through April is crappie season; they can be found along the lower half of the lake. Mini-jigs, worms and minnows are the ticket for catching them. A wheelchair-accessible fishing dock is located at Katherine Landing. **Note:** There is a multiagency effort under way to protect endangered species of the Colorado River. Fishermen should identify and immediately release humpback chubs, bonytail chubs, razorback suckers and Colorado squawfish that they hook. Anglers who are unfamiliar with these species will find descriptions in the California and Arizona fishing regulations booklets that are available where licenses are sold.

Swimming

Lake Mohave offers swimming, snorkeling and diving in clear waters. Except for the northern reaches of the lake, where the water is quite cold, the water averages about 78 degrees during spring, summer and fall.

Water-Skiing

Water-skiing is permitted on all of Lake Mohave except along a 21-mile stretch of the Colorado River extending south from Hoover Dam to Chalk Cliffs.

Below Davis Dam

Accessible via Ariz SR 95. Elevation 550. This stretch of the Colorado River is bordered by mobile home parks and the many casinos of Laughlin, Nevada. Activities include swimming, water-skiing, sailboarding, use of personal watercraft and fishing. Supplies and tourist facilities are available in Bullhead City and Laughlin, and boat launching ramps are scattered along the shoreline.

Boating

BULLHEAD CITY ROTARY PARK *2315 Balboa Dr, Bullhead City, Ariz. (928) 763-9400 ext 114. Open daily. $10 entry fee May 26 through Sep.* Paved launch ramp. Picnic area.

DAVIS CAMP COUNTY PARK *Mohave County Park, Bullhead City, Ariz. (928) 754-4606. Open daily. $4 entry fee.* Paved launch ramp, dry storage. Ice, tent and RV sites, picnic area.

LAZY HARRY'S *Off Whitewater Dr; 2170 Rio Grande Rd, Bullhead City, Ariz. (928) 758-6322. Open daily.* Paved launch ramp. Ice, restaurant, picnic area.

Fishing

Rainbow trout are the most popular catch along this stretch of the river; they inhabit the cold water along the gravel beds below Davis Dam (no fishing in posted areas). Trout are also planted south of Laughlin-Bullhead City near the California-Nevada state line from October to June. During warm weather, the fish are attracted to lures such as Super Dupers, Panther Martins, and spinners and spoons. In cooler weather, the best bet is live bait, mostly night crawlers and marshmallow combos. The fish stay in deep water during the day and move toward shore at night.

Anglers can also fill their creels with good-sized catfish, largemouth bass, and plenty of bluegill and crappie. Bass prefer the cooler deep water and will hit on live bait or floating lures. Catfish like stink baits (garlic cheese), dough balls, anchovies and night crawlers. Bluegill and crappie hit on almost anything that moves—try worms for bluegill, and minnows or mini-jigs for crappie.

Striped bass are a popular game fish, and they often tip the scales at around 30 pounds. The largest striper ever caught in an inland habitat was landed at Bullhead City and weighed in at 59 pounds, 12 ounces. These fish winter at Lake Havasu and start moving north in the spring, hitting the Laughlin-Bullhead City area in May; common baits are shad, frozen anchovies or sardines, with sinkers to keep the bait below the surface of the water.

Inner Tubing

Inner tubing is a popular sport along the Colorado River. For easy pickup and parking, swimmers usually launch their inner tubes from Davis Camp County Park, north of Bullhead City, Arizona, and float four or five miles south along the river, disembarking at Bullhead Community Park.

Swimming

Swimming in the river should not be attempted except from designated beach areas. A public beach is located at Davis Camp County Park on the Arizona side of the river (north of Bullhead City on SR 95). The best swimming in the area is at Lake

♠ Houseboating

Houseboats are permitted on Lake Mead, Lake Mohave and on the 75-mile stretch of the Colorado River from Davis Dam south to Parker Dam. There are 246 square miles of uncrowded, open waters for houseboaters on Lake Mead. The numerous secluded coves and scenic steep-walled canyons along its 550 miles of shoreline make the area popular with boaters. The Colorado River section from Davis Dam south offers varied scenery, including rugged mountains, marshes, a narrow canyon (south of Needles) and the wide expanse of Lake Havasu. Lake Mohave has numerous coves and inlets to explore at the south end of the lake, including many sandy coves. The mild winter weather and hot summer days make houseboating popular all year in each of these areas; however, summer thunderstorms are common. Reservations should be made well in advance. Houseboats can be rented at the following locations—Lake Mead: Callville Bay Resort and Marina, (800) 255-5561; Lake Mead Arena, Temple Bar Resorts and Echo Bay Resort, (800) 752-9669. Lake Mohave: Cottonwood Cove Resort and Marina, (800) 255-5561; Lake Mohave Resort, (800) 752-9669.

Mohave. In the summer the lake water can get as warm as 80 degrees. **Note:** A word of caution to river swimmers south of Davis Dam—the water released from the dam is very cold, about 60 degrees.

Water-Skiing

Water-skiing is allowed along the Colorado River from Bullhead City south to Needles. A sparsely populated area just south of Bullhead City is usually the best location for the sport.

Transportation

A rich variety of transportation choices to Las Vegas and Laughlin make getting there easy for conventioneers, families and groups of singles. Both desert cities boast international airports, convenient bus service and well-maintained roads.

Air

For complete schedule information and help arranging flights from cities with direct or connecting service, contact any **AAA Travel Agency** office. Members in Southern California can call (800) 222-5000, Monday through Friday from 8 a.m. to 6 p.m., and Saturday from 9 a.m. to 1 p.m.

LAUGHLIN/BULLHEAD INTERNATIONAL AIRPORT *2550 Laughlin View Dr, Bullhead City, AZ. (928) 754-2134.* This $23 million airport is located in Arizona just minutes from the casino gaming action across the river. The 7500-foot-by-150-foot runway accommodates aircraft as large as DC-10s, and is served by two commuter airlines and three charter carriers. About 100 flights are logged each week, serving more than 230,000 passengers a year. Taxis and free hotel shuttles serve the airport, and several car rental agencies have offices here.

McCARRAN INTERNATIONAL AIRPORT *1 mile from the Las Vegas Strip; 5757 Wayne Newton Blvd, Las Vegas. (702) 261-5211; TDD (702) 261-3111.* McCarran is the 10th-busiest airport in the North America and 16th-busiest in the world, with more than 33 million passengers passing through it each year. More than 60 air carriers serve Las Vegas, among them 23 scheduled airlines, two commuter lines and up to 20 charter airlines (depending on the season). The airport also provides international service to Belgium, Canada, Germany, Japan, Mexico and the United Kingdom, all of which adds up to some 800 commercial and chartered flights a day.

As Las Vegas' tourism industry grows, so must the ancillary structures that support tourism. The airport, for example, has experienced a 77 percent increase in passenger traffic since 1990. In order to accommodate this increase as well as to provide room for future anticipated growth, a use plan has been developed for McCarran International Airport that will guide it well into the 21st century. The most recent expansion was the opening of the new "D" Gates. These additional gates will allow McCarran to serve 45 million passengers annually.

McCarran International Airport serves more than 33 million passengers annually.

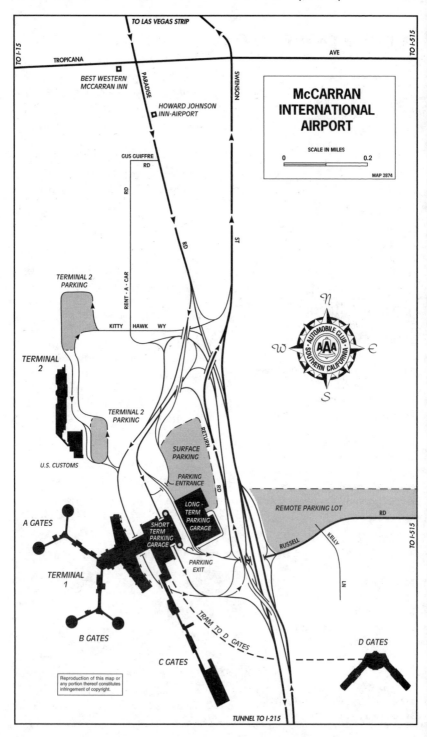

Private shuttle buses, taxis, limousines and public buses make pickups at McCarran. The Citizens Area Transit (CAT) buses numbered "108" and "109" serve the airport; call (702) 228-7433 for further details. Ground transportation services at McCarran are abundant; see the Las Vegas telephone directory yellow pages under "Airport Transportation & Parking Services." All major car rental companies have offices at McCarran; refer to the yellow pages under "Automobile Renting and Leasing." Any AAA Travel Agency can help arrange reservations for a car rental.

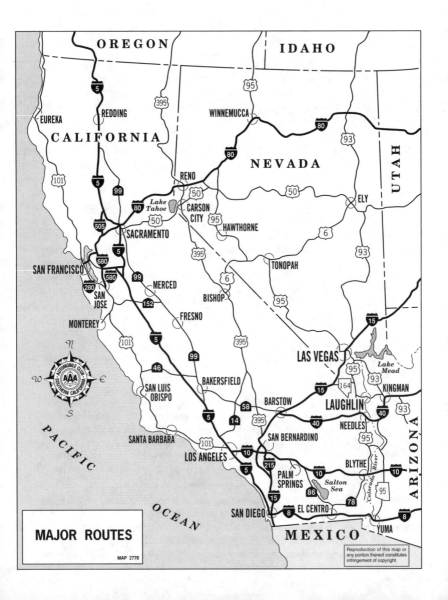

MAJOR ROUTES

MAP 2778

♠ Desert Driving Hints

Regardless of the point of departure, any automobile trip from California to Las Vegas will involve some desert driving. At all times, but especially during the summer months, some basic precautions should be taken when planning to cross the Mojave Desert.

- Check the condition of your car's engine and cooling systems and make sure they're in good working order. Look closely for radiator leaks, worn fan belts and cracked hoses.

- Take about five gallons of water in a clean container for emergency purposes—both for the car's radiator and for drinking. If your car overheats, do not remove the radiator cap immediately because of the risk of explosion. After the engine has cooled, slowly remove the cap and add water, leaving about an inch of air space between the water level and the top of the radiator. If an older model car experiences vapor lock, wrap a wet towel around the gas line between the fuel pump and the carburetor. Caution should be used in order to insure that the towel does not become entangled in any moving parts (belts). This may cool the line and allow the car to start.

- Make certain that your car's tires are properly inflated before starting out. If the tires become overly hard while crossing the desert, do not release any air. Instead, stop the car and allow the tires to cool, then proceed. Before setting out, inspect the spare tire and inflate to proper pressure.

- Watch the gasoline gauge and buy fuel when it is available. Towns in the Mojave Desert are few and far between; don't get stuck without gas and no place to purchase it.

- If your car becomes disabled, once safely out of the traffic lane activate the hazard warning lights and raise your hood. Do not abandon the car to go for help. Not only is it often a long walk to the nearest town or telephone, but extreme desert temperatures in the summer months bring a real threat of heat stroke—even a short walk could become dangerous.

Note: Desert driving often means that travelers must take "out of the ordinary" precautions in an emergency. For instance, pulling your car as far off the road as possible in an emergency is usually the most desirable action to take. Many areas of desert terrain do not offer a firm gravel surface off the asphalt shoulder, however, so be aware that driving onto a shoulder of soft sand may mean a tow truck will be required to get your car back onto the road.

When weather permits, motorists should follow normal emergency procedures: remain in your car, in the seat that is the farthest from moving traffic, keep the seat belt fastened and headrest properly positioned, keep doors locked and wait for assistance. In extreme desert heat these procedures will not be possible—even with the windows rolled down, the car will become unbearably hot. In such cases, seek out a shady area to wait for highway assistance, either in the shadow of the vehicle itself or in the shade of nearby vegetation. Do not leave pets or children in the car—they suffer the effects of the heat even more quickly than adults.

When faced with a disabled car, the best course of action the Auto Club can recommend is to wait for Highway Patrol assistance. Emergency call boxes are numerous along well-traveled highways, and cellular phones can be convenient tools for getting swift assistance. Highway Patrol officers also routinely make regular patrols of desert highways. Motorists should use extreme caution in accepting help from strangers.

Automobile

Las Vegas entertains millions of visitors each year, and not surprisingly more than half of them arrive by automobile. More than 4 million people a year drive to Nevada's largest city from the state of California. Southern Californians account for most of the automobile traffic. With the 70 mph speed limit in effect on I-15, Las Vegas is only about a 5½-hour drive from Los Angeles; from San Diego it is about an hour farther. The San Francisco Bay Area is some 11 hours away by car, exclusive of stops. Although the 70 mph speed limit is in effect for almost all of the driving along I-15 in both California and Nevada, weather and road conditions often dictate a lower speed. For current highway conditions, call the Nevada Department of Transportation at (702) 486-3116 (recording); in California call (800) 927-7623. Drivers should also be alert to posted lower speed limits in populated areas.

Laughlin is approximately the same distance from Los Angeles as Las Vegas. The routes from Los Angeles to both Las Vegas and Laughlin begin in a similar manner: I-10 east past Ontario, then north on I-15 to Barstow. At Barstow those bound for Las Vegas continue on I-15. For Laughlin, motorists take I-40 east across the Mojave Desert toward Needles. Near Needles there are two possible routes for the remainder of the drive to Laughlin: about 10 miles west of Needles motorists can take US 95 north 24 miles, then take SR 163 east 18 miles to Laughlin Civic Drive; or about four miles west of Needles, there's an alternate route along Needles Highway (River Road) north to Laughlin. To get to the Arizona side of the river, SR 95 and Bullhead City, there's a choice of three bridges (listed south to north): Needles, Veterans and Laughlin. For **emergency roadside assistance**, AAA members may call **(800) AAA-HELP** in the USA and Canada; hearing impaired call **(800) 464-0889**.

Bus

Greyhound/Trailways offers service to Las Vegas from virtually any town in California and Nevada. Reservations are not accepted, and tickets can usually be purchased just prior to departure. In Las Vegas, Greyhound/Trailways uses the downtown bus terminal building at 200 South Main Street (at Carson Avenue); phone (800) 231-2222.

The route for bus travelers to Laughlin-Bullhead City is through Needles, California, or Las Vegas, Nevada. From there, both Greyhound/Trailways and K-T Services bus lines provide daily service to Laughlin; the trip takes about 2½ hours. Don Laughlin's Riverside Resort Hotel & Casino, South Tower, is the terminus in Laughlin for both bus lines. Both companies also serve Bullhead City, with pickups and drop-offs at the River Queen Motel, 125 Long Street. For more information, phone Greyhound/Trailways at (702) 298-1934 or (800) 231-2222, or K-T Services at (702) 644-2233.

Train

As of press time, Amtrak was planning to start daily, round-trip service along the Los Angeles-Las Vegas route in the spring of 2003. *Anticipated departure times: eastbound from Los Angeles, 9:30 a.m.; westbound from Las Vegas, 4 p.m. As of press time, prices had not been established.* Custom designed trains will make the 340-mile trip in approximately 5½ hours, with one intermediate stop in Montclair. The single-level trains are decorated on the outside in Nevada's state colors of silver and blue and on the inside with purple, orange, fuchsia and teal. These are the first Amtrak trains that will allow guests in wheelchairs the option of moving from the passenger cars to the bistro or dining cars.

For fare and schedule information, call Amtrak at (800) 872-7245. For reservations and help in arranging connecting trains or buses, contact any AAA Travel Agency.

Tourist Information Services

The chambers of commerce and visitor information bureaus listed below are resources for obtaining additional information about Las Vegas, Laughlin and the surrounding areas. AAA/CSAA district offices provide travel services and publications, and highway information to Auto Club members.

Chambers of Commerce & Visitor Information Bureaus

Boulder City Chamber of Commerce
1305 Arizona St, Boulder City, NV
(702) 293-2034
Office hours: Mon-Fri 9 am-5 pm

Bullhead Area Chamber of Commerce
1251 Hwy 95, Bullhead City, AZ
(928) 754-4121
Office hours: Mon-Fri 9 am-5 pm

Las Vegas Convention and Visitors Authority
3150 Paradise Rd, Las Vegas, NV
(702) 892-7575, 892-0711
Office hours: Mon-Fri 8 am-5 pm

Laughlin Visitors Bureau
1555 S Casino Dr, Laughlin, NV
(702) 298-3321
Office hours: Daily 8 am-4:30 pm

Nevada Welcome Center
100 Nevada Hwy, Boulder City, NV
(702) 294-1252
Office hours: Daily 8:00 am-4:30 pm

Auto Club District Offices

AAA Travel Agencies can help members in preparing a trip to anywhere in the world. For travel within the United States, Canada and Mexico, the Club can make reservations for lodging and transportation, and provide weather, routing and emergency road service information. They can make airline, train and package tour reservations for travel throughout the world.

Auto Club members can also take advantage of discounts on lodging, as indicated in the AAA *Southern California & Las Vegas TourBook*, available free to members. Auto Club members in Southern California can take advantage of the *Member Saver*, which is published monthly and is a valuable source for seasonal discounts on events and points of interest.

The following AAA/California State Automobile Association district offices are located in the Las Vegas region.

Henderson
601-A Whitney Ranch Dr, Henderson, NV
(702) 458-2323
Office hours: Mon-Fri 8:30 am- 5:30 pm

Las Vegas
3312 W Charleston Blvd, Las Vegas, NV
(702) 870-9171
Office hours: Mon-Fri 8:30 am-5:30 pm

Summerlin
8440 W Lake Mead, Ste 203, Las Vegas, NV
(702) 360-3151
Office hours: Mon-Fri 8:30 am-5:30 pm

Lodging & Restaurants

*Despite the fact that **Las Vegas** has more than 120,000 rooms, it is advisable to make reservations as far in advance as possible. "No vacancy" signs are constant reminders that the town generally operates at near capacity all year. Although economic and travel uncertainties can take their toll here the same as anywhere, under normal conditions a one-night reservation for Friday or Saturday night is difficult to obtain.*

There are several things to be considered in addition to price when staying in Las Vegas. It is easier to obtain reservations to sellout celebrity shows when staying at the hotel where the performer is appearing. If convenient parking is important, a motel would probably be preferable to a hotel. Golf privileges, tennis and spa facilities may also be a consideration.

***Laughlin** draws more than 50,000 visitors to its casinos on an average weekend, and holiday crowds can be even larger. While space is limited in Laughlin, additional lodging can also be found across the river in **Bullhead City, Arizona** (listings follow Nevada cities). Passenger ferries provide frequent service from parking lots on the Arizona side of the river to the various casinos on the Nevada side, and 24-hour shuttle bus service is available between the two cities.*

*Lodgings and restaurants are listed alphabetically by city and also include the communities of **Boulder City, Cottonwood Cove, Echo Bay-Lake Mead, Henderson** and **Primm**.*

A trained representative of AAA has inspected the properties listed in these pages at least once in the past year. In surprise inspections, each property was found to meet AAA's extensive and detailed requirements for approval. These requirements are reflective of current industry standards and the expectations of the traveling public. Properties are listed alphabetically under the nearest town, with lodging facilities first and restaurants second. Each facility's location is given from the center of town or from the nearest major highway.

Most listings include AAA's "diamond" rating, reflecting the overall quality of the establishment. Many factors are considered in the process of determining the diamond rating. In lodging properties, the facility is first "classified" according to its physical design—is it a motel, a hotel, a resort, an apartment, etc. Since the various types of lodging establishments offer differing amenities and facilities, rating criteria are specific for each classification. For example, a motel, which typically offers a room with convenient parking and few if any recreational or public facilities, is rated using criteria designed only for motel-type establishments—it is not compared to a hotel with its extensive public and meeting areas, or to a resort with its wide range of recreational facilities and programs. The diamonds do, however, represent standard levels of quality in all types of establishments.

There is no charge for a property to be listed in AAA publications. However, many lodgings and restaurants have expressed a special desire to attract the

AAA member's business. In order to communicate this interest to the traveling public, these facilities have purchased the right to display the Ⓐ. As a service to our members, these listings may include more information.

Nearly all lodging and restaurant facilities accept credit cards as forms of payment for services rendered. The following symbols are used to identify the specific cards accepted by each property: AE=American Express, CB=Carte Blanche, DI=Diners Club, DS=Discover, MC=MasterCard, VI=VISA.

Listings which denote "laundry" may offer a coin laundry, valet laundry and/or dry cleaning service. The term "business services" indicates that any of these are available: personal computers, administrative or secretarial services, and meeting rooms and/or conference facilities. Call the establishment to determine if the services and/or facilities you require are offered.

Some lodgings and restaurants listed in Auto Club publications have symbols indicating that they are accessible to individuals with disabilities. The criteria used in qualifying these listings are consistent with, but do not represent the full scope of, the Americans with Disabilities Act of 1990 Accessibility Guidelines (ADAAG). AAA does not evaluate recreational facilities, banquet rooms, or convention and meeting facilities for accessibility. Individuals with disabilities are urged to phone ahead to fully understand an establishment's accessibility options.

In accommodations, a 🅖 indicates that at least one fully accessible guest room exists and that an individual with mobility impairments will be able to park and enter the building, register, and use at least one food and beverage outlet. For restaurants, the symbol indicates that parking, dining rooms and restrooms are accessible.

The 🆉 in a lodging listing means that the following in-room elements are provided: closed-captioned decoders; text telephones; visual notification for fire alarms, incoming phone calls and door knocks; and phone amplification devices.

Lodging

The following accommodation's classifications may appear in this book.

Apartment—Usually four or more stories with at least half the units equipped for housekeeping. Often in a vacation destination area. Units typically provide a full kitchen, living room and one or more bedrooms, but may be studio-type rooms with kitchen equipment in an alcove. May require a minimum stay and/or offer discounts for longer stays. This classification may also modify any of the other lodging types.

Complex—A combination of two or more kinds of lodgings.

Condominium—A destination property located in a resort area. Guest units consist of a bedroom, living room and kitchen. Kitchens are separate from bedrooms and are equipped with a stove, oven or microwave, refrigerator, cooking utensils and table settings for the maximum number of people occupying the unit. Linens and maid service are provided at least twice weekly. This classification may also modify any of the other lodging types.

Extended Stay—A property that caters to long-term visits. The guest unit will have a kitchen or efficiency, and may have a separate living room area, evening office, and limited housekeeping services.

Hotel—A multistory building usually including a coffee shop, dining room, lounge, room service, convenience shops, valet, laundry and full banquet/meeting facilities. Parking may be limited.

Motel—Usually one or two stories; food service, if any, consists of a limited facility or snack bar. Often has a pool or playground. Ample parking, usually adjacent to the guest room.

Motor Inn—Usually two or three stories, but may be a high-rise. Generally has recreation facilities, food service and ample parking. May have limited banquet/meeting facilities.

Resort—May be a destination in itself. Has a vacation atmosphere offering extensive recreational facilities for such specific interests as golf, tennis, fishing, etc. Rates may include meals under American or Modified American plans. This classification may also modify any of the other lodging types.

Suite—Units have one or more bedrooms and a living room which may or may not be closed off from the bedrooms. This classification modifies other lodging types.

A property's diamond rating is not based on the room rate or any one specific aspect of its facilities or operations. Many factors are considered in calculating the rating, and certain minimum standards must be met in all inspection categories. If a property fails approval in just one category, it does not receive a AAA diamond rating. The inspection categories include housekeeping, maintenance, service, furnishings and decor. Guest comments received by AAA may also be reviewed in a property's approval/rating process.

These criteria apply to all properties listed in this publication:

- Clean and well-maintained facilities
- Hospitable staff
- Adequate parking
- A well-kept appearance
- Good quality bedding and comfortable beds, with adequate illumination
- Good locks on all doors and windows
- Comfortable furnishings and decor
- Smoke detectors
- Adequate towels and supplies
- At least one comfortable easy chair with adequate illumination
- A desk or other writing surface with adequate illumination

Lodging ratings range from one to five diamonds and are defined below:

♦—Good but unpretentious. Establishments are functional. Clean and comfortable rooms must meet the basic needs of privacy and cleanliness.

♦♦—Shows noticeable enhancements in decor and/or quality of furnishings over those at the one-diamond level. May be recently constructed or an older property. Targets the needs of a budget-oriented traveler.

♦♦♦—Offers a degree of sophistication with additional amenities, services and facilities. There is a marked upgrade in services and comfort.

♦♦♦♦—Excellent properties displaying high levels of service and hospitality, and offering a wide variety of amenities and upscale facilities, inside the room, on the grounds and in the common areas.

♦♦♦♦♦—Renowned for an exceptionally high degree of service, attractive and luxurious facilities, and many extra amenities. Guest services are executed and presented in a flawless manner. Guests are pampered by a very professional, attentive staff. The property's facilities and operations set standards in hospitality and service.

The diamond ratings shown in this publication are based on inspections done in 1999-00. Occasionally a property is listed without a rating, such as when an establishment was under construction or undergoing renovations at press time and a rating could not be determined.

Room rates shown in the listings are provided by each establishment's management for publication by AAA. Rates range from the minimum off-season rate to the maximum high-season rate, for one or two persons occupying a typical room as opposed to a special unit. Taxes are not included. **All rates are subject to change.** During special events or holiday periods, rates may exceed those published, and special discounts or savings programs may not be honored. Most rates listed are European plan, which means that no meals are included in the rate. You'll need to inquire as to whether a lodging's rates include breakfast or continental breakfast. Our listings do not indicate the availability of special meal plans, such as American Plan, which includes three meals, or Modified American Plan, which offers two meals, usually breakfast and dinner.

Many properties make special and discounted rates available exclusively to AAA members. Two publications list these rates: the AAA *TourBook*, which is published annually, and the Auto Club's *Member Saver*, a monthly newsletter featuring short-term rates and packages that offer discounts for reservations made through the Auto Club. AAA *TourBooks* are available to AAA members at no charge through AAA offices; the Member Saver is available to AAA members at no charge through all Automobile Club of Southern California district offices.

Some properties offer discounts to senior citizens, or special rate periods such as weekly or monthly rentals. Inquiries as to the availability of any special discounts should be made at the time of registration. Typically, a property will allow a guest to take advantage of only one discount during his or her stay (i.e., a guest staying at a property offering both a AAA discount and a senior discount may choose only one of the two savings plans).

Since nearly all establishments have air conditioning, telephones and color cable TV, only the absence of any of these items is noted in the listing. Other facilities, amenities and services, such as movies, in-room whirlpool, child care, massage and recreational activities, may have extra fees associated with them. It is best to inquire about these fees when making reservations. Check-in time is shown only if it is after 3 p.m.; check-out time is shown only if it is before 10 a.m. Service charges are not shown unless they are $1 or more, or at least 5 percent of the room rate. If the pet acceptance policy varies within the establishment, no mention of pets is made; it is best to call ahead to verify specifics. By U.S. law, pet restrictions do not apply to service animals. Outdoor pools may or may not be heated, and may not be open in winter.

Reservations are always advisable in resort areas and may be the only way to assure obtaining the type of accommodations desired. Deposits are almost always required. Should plans change and reservations need to be canceled, be aware of the amount of notice required to receive a deposit refund.

Many properties welcome children in the same room with their parents at no additional charge; individual listings indicate if there is an age limit. There may be charges for additional equipment, such as roll-aways or cribs. Some properties offer a discount for guests ages 60 and over—be aware that the senior discount cannot usually be taken in conjunction with or in addition to other discounts. Many establishments have a minimum age requirement for renting rooms; in most cases the minimum age is 18, but at some properties the minimum age is 21.

In order to be listed, facilities must have smoke detectors and may have additional fire safety equipment. Listings here do not reference these items. Members should call the facility in order to obtain more detailed fire-safety information. Many properties have reserved rooms for nonsmokers; look for the ⊘ symbol in the listing. If a smoke-free room is desired, be sure to request it when making a reservation and upon registration.

Restaurants

Restaurants listed in this publication have been found to be consistently good dining establishments. In metropolitan areas, where many restaurants are above average, some of those known for the superiority of their food, service and atmosphere are selected, as well as those offering a selection of quality food at moderate prices (including some cafeterias and family restaurants). In smaller communities, the restaurants considered to be the best in the area may be listed.

The type of cuisine featured at a dining establishment is used as a means of classification for restaurants. There are listings for Steakhouses and Continental cuisine as well as a range of ethnic foods, such as Brazilian, French, Italian and yes, American. Special menu types, such as early bird, a la carte, children's or Sunday brunch, are also listed. In many cases something is indicated about each restaurant's atmosphere and appropriate attire. The availability of alcoholic beverages is shown, as well as entertainment and dancing.

Price ranges are for an average, complete meal without alcoholic beverage. Taxes and tips are not included.

Restaurant ratings are applied to two categories of operational style—full-service eating establishments, and self-service, family-dining operations such as cafeterias or buffets.

♦—Good but unpretentious dishes. Table settings are usually simple and may include paper place mats and napkins. Alcoholic beverage service, if any, may be limited to beer and wine. Usually informal with an atmosphere conducive to family dining.

♦♦—More extensive menus representing more complex food preparation and, usually, a wider variety of alcoholic beverages. The atmosphere is appealing and suitable for either family or adult dining. Service may be casual, but host or hostess seating can be expected. Table settings may include tablecloths and cloth napkins.

♦♦♦—Extensive or specialized menus and more complex cuisine preparation requiring that a professional chef contribute to either a formal dining experience or a special family meal. Cloth table linens, above-average quality table settings, a skilled service staff and an inviting decor should all be provided. Generally, the wine list includes representatives of the best domestic and foreign wine-producing regions.

♦♦♦♦—An appealing ambiance is often enhanced by fresh flowers and fine furnishings. The overall sophistication and formal atmosphere visually create a dining experience more for adults than for families. The wine list, as well as the staff's knowledge about wine, is more extensive than that of a three-diamond restaurant. A smartly attired, highly skilled staff is capable of describing how any dish is prepared. Elegant silverware, china and correct glassware are typical. The menu includes creative dishes prepared from fresh ingredients by a chef who frequently has international training. Eye-appealing desserts are offered at tableside.

♦♦♦♦♦—A world-class operation with even more luxury and sophistication than four-diamond restaurants. A proportionally large staff, expert in preparing tableside delicacies, provides flawless service. Tables are set with impeccable linens, silver and crystal glassware.

♠ Dining Out

Dining in **Las Vegas** is as varied as accommodations. Prices range from less than $1 for breakfast to more than $50 for gourmet dinners. All of the large hotels have several places to eat, and many have themed dining rooms that feature regional or ethnic decor and food. Many coffee shops are open 24 hours. Buffets are available at almost every major hotel and offer diners a choice of three or four entrees, plus potatoes, vegetables, salads, desserts and a beverage for one price; buffet-style champagne brunches are offered at numerous hotels on weekends.

Similarly, all the large casino/hotels in Laughlin have several restaurants, some with themed dining rooms overlooking the river, that feature regional or ethnic foods. Also, a number of restaurants and major fast-food franchise outlets can be found across the river in Bullhead City. Prices in Laughlin range from a low of about $2 for breakfast to a high of $70 for a gourmet dinner. Buffets are common and range in price from $5 to $7, with buffet breakfasts priced from $2 to $3.50 and lunches priced similarly.

Boulder City

Lodging

BEST WESTERN LIGHTHOUSE INN ⓐ ♦♦ Motel
(702) 293-6444 Rates not provided
1 mi E via SR 93; 110 Ville Dr.
Continental breakfast. AE, CB, DI, DS, MC, VI. Pets, $10 fee. 3 stories; exterior corridors; no elevator. **Rooms:** 70. Some whirlpools, ⊘. **Recreation:** Pools, whirlpool, pools. **Services:** Laundry, business services.

EL RANCHO BOULDER MOTEL ⓐ ♦♦ Motel
(702) 293-1085 Rates not provided
On US 93; 725 Nevada Hwy.
AE, CB, DI, DS, MC, VI. 2 stories; exterior corridors. **Rooms:** 39. ⊘ **Recreation:** Pools.

SANDS MOTEL ⓐ ♦ Motel
(702) 293-2589 $47-53
On US 93; 809 Nevada Hwy.
XP $6. 3-day refund notice. AE, CB, DI, DS, MC, VI. 1 story; exterior corridors. **Rooms:** 25. Some shower baths, ⊘.

SUPER 8 MOTEL ♦ Motel
(702) 294-8888 $45-140
On US 93; 704 Nevada Hwy.
XP $5. AE, CB, DI, DS, MC, VI. Small pets only, $8 fee. 3 stories; exterior corridors. **Rooms:** 114. Some shower baths, some whirlpools, ⊘. **Recreation:** Whirlpool, pools. **Services:** Laundry, business services.

Cottonwood Cove

Lodging

COTTONWOOD COVE MOTEL ⓐ ♦♦ Motel
(702) 297-1464 $60-95
Between Las Vegas and Needles; 14 mi E of Searchlight, off US 95; 1000 Cottonwood Cove Rd.
XP $10. 14-day refund notice; cancellation fee. AE, DS, MC, VI. Gift shop, gas station, general store. 1 story; exterior corridors. **Rooms:** 24. **Recreation:** Marina, fishing, water-skiing, powerboats and equipment. **Services:** Laundry. **Dining:** Coffee shop; 7 am-8 pm, 11/1-4/1 to 6 pm; $7-12.

Echo Bay-Lake Mead

Lodging

ECHO BAY RESORT ⓐ ♦♦ Motor Inn
(702) 394-4000 $60-115
On Lake Mead; 4 mi E of SR 167.

XP $6. 3-day refund notice. DS, MC, VI. Pets, $5 extra charge. Gift shop. 2 stories; interior corridors. **Rooms:** 52. **Recreation:** Marina, fishing, water-skiing, rental boats. **Services:** Laundry, business services. **Dining:** Restaurant; 7 am-8:30 pm, 10/1-4/5 10 am-4 pm; $8-17; cocktails.

Henderson

Lodging

BEST WESTERN LAKE MEAD MOTEL ⏺   ♦♦ Motel
(702) 564-1712   Rates not provided
US 93/95, exit Lake Mead Dr; 1½ mi E on SR 146; 85 W Lake Mead Dr.
Continental breakfast. AE, CB, DI, DS, MC, VI. 2 stories; exterior corridors. **Rooms:** 59. Some shower baths, ⊘. **Recreation:** Pools. **Services:** Laundry.

HAMPTON INN HOTEL & SUITES   ♦♦♦ Motel
(702) 992-9292   Rates not provided
421 Astaire Dr.
AE, DI, DS, MC, VI. 3 stories; interior corridors. **Rooms:** 99. Some shower baths. **Recreation:** Pools, whirlpool, exercise room. **Services:** Laundry, business services.

HAWTHORN INN & SUITES ⏺   ♦♦♦ Hotel
(702) 568-7800 $79-160
910 S Boulder Hwy.
XP $10. Continental breakfast. Cancellation fee. AE, CB, DI, DS, MC, VI. Pets; $15 deposit. Gift shop. 3 stories; interior corridors. **Rooms:** 71. Some shower baths, some whirlpools, ⊘. Roll-in showers. **Recreation:** Pools, whirlpool, exercise room. **Services:** Laundry, business services.

HOLIDAY INN EXPRESS & SUITES   ♦♦♦ Motel
(702) 990-2323   Rates not provided
441 Astaire Dr.
AE, CB, DI, DS, MC, VI. 3 stories; interior/exterior corridors. **Rooms:** 101. Some shower baths, high-speed Internet. **Recreation:** Pools, whirlpool, exercise room. **Services:** Laundry, business services.

HYATT REGENCY LAKE LAS VEGAS RESORT   ♦♦♦♦ Hotel
(702) 567-1234   Rates not provided
101 Montelago Bl.
AE, CB, DI, DS, MC, VI. Gift shop. 9 stories; interior corridors. **Rooms:** 496. Some shower baths, some whirlpools, safes. **Recreation:** Pools, whirlpool, exercise room, massage, canoe and paddleboat rentals, bicycles. **Services:** Valet parking, laundry, business services.

THE RESERVE HOTEL CASINO   ♦♦♦ Hotel
(702) 558-7000   Rates not provided
I-515 exit Lake Mead Dr; 777 W Lake Mead Dr.
AE, CB, DI, DS, MC, VI. Gift shop. 9 stories; interior corridors. **Rooms:** 224. Some shower baths, some whirlpools, video games, ⊘. ▨ **Recreation:** Pools, whirlpool. **Services:** Laundry, business services.

RESIDENCE INN-GREEN VALLEY   ♦♦♦ Motel
(702) 434-2700   Rates not provided
I-215 exit Green Valley Pkwy N; 2190 Olympic Av.
AE, CB, DI, DS, MC, VI. Pets, $50 fee; $10 extra charge. 3 stories; interior corridors. **Rooms:** 126. Some shower baths, some kitchens. **Recreation:** Whirlpool, pools, exercise room, sports court. **Services:** Laundry, business services.

SUNSET STATION HOTEL & CASINO ⒶⒶ   ♦♦♦ Hotel
(702) 547-7777   Rates not provided
I-15 at I-215 exit to Warm Springs; 7 mi E to Stephanie and Sunset Rd; 1301 W Sunset Rd.
AE, DI, DS, MC, VI. Gift shop. Casino, movie complex. 21 stories; interior corridors. **Rooms:** 457. Some shower baths, some whirlpools, safes, ⊘. Roll-in showers, ▨. **Recreation:** Pools, exercise room. **Services:** Area transportation, laundry, business services. **Dining:** 4 dining rooms; 3 restaurants; coffee shop; buffet; 24 hrs; $18-35; cocktails; nightclub.

Las Vegas

Lodging

ALEXIS PARK RESORT HOTEL   ♦♦♦ Hotel
(702) 796-3300   Rates not provided
I-15 exit Tropicana Av; 2 blks W to UNLV, 2 mi S of convention center; 375 E Harmon Av.
AE, CB, DI, DS, MC, VI. Gift shop. 2 stories; exterior corridors. **Rooms:** 496. Some whirlpools, ⊘. ▨ **Recreation:** Pools, saunas, whirlpools, massage. **Services:** Valet parking, laundry, business services.

AMERISUITES LAS VEGAS ⒶⒶ   ♦♦♦ Motel
(702) 369-3366   Rates not provided
Cross sts Harmon and Paradise, E of the Strip; 4520 Paradise Av.
Continental breakfast. AE, CB, DI, DS, MC, VI. Small pets only. 6 stories; interior corridors. **Rooms:** 202. Some shower baths, high-speed Internet, video games, ⊘. Roll-in showers, ▨. **Recreation:** Pools, exercise room. **Services:** Area transportation, laundry, business services.

ARIZONA CHARLIE'S HOTEL   ♦♦ Motor Inn
(702) 258-5200   Rates not provided
I-15 exit Charleston Bl W, 7 mi NW; 740 S Decatur Bl, Evergreen Av.
AE, CB, DI, DS, MC, VI. Gift shop. 3-7 stories; interior corridors. **Rooms:** 257. Some shower baths, some whirlpools, ⊘. ▤, roll-in showers, ▨. **Recreation:** Pools, whirlpool. **Services:** Valet parking, laundry, business services.

BALLY'S LAS VEGAS   ♦♦♦ Hotel
(702) 739-4111   Rates not provided
4½ mi S on the Strip; 3645 Las Vegas Bl S.
AE, CB, DI, DS, MC, VI. Gift shop. 26 stories; interior corridors. **Rooms:** 2814. Some shower baths, safes, ⊘. Roll-in showers, ▨. **Recreation:** Pools, sauna, whirlpool, steam room, massage, 8 lighted tennis courts. **Services:** Valet parking, laundry, business services. **Dining:** See listing for Al Dente.

BARBARY COAST HOTEL 🏧

♦♦♦ Hotel

(702) 737-7111 Rates not provided
1¾ mi S on the Strip; 3595 Las Vegas Bl S.
AE, CB, DI, DS, MC, VI. Gift shop. 5 stories; interior corridors. **Rooms:** 200. Shower baths, some whirlpools, ⊘. Roll-in showers, 🔲. **Services:** Valet parking, laundry. **Dining:** 2 restaurants (see listing for Michaels); coffee shop; $12-80; 24 hrs; cocktails.

BARCELONA MOTEL 🏧

♦♦ Motor Inn

(702) 644-6300 Rates not provided
I-15 exit 48 eastbound, 7 mi NE; ½ mi from Nellis AFB; 5011 E Craig Rd.
AE, DS, MC, VI. Small casino. 2 stories; exterior corridors. **Rooms:** 172. Some shower baths, safes, ⊘. Roll-in showers. **Recreation:** Whirlpool. **Services:** Laundry, business services. **Dining:** Coffee shop; $5-10; 24 hrs; cocktails.

BELLAGIO 🏧

♦♦♦♦ Hotel

(702) 693-7111 $159-899
I-15 exit E Flamingo Av, on the Strip; 3600 Las Vegas Bl S.
XP $35. AE, CB, DI, DS, MC, VI. Gift shop, casino. Exquisite exterior and public areas including water fountains, conservatory, glass-sculptured lobby ceiling, art gallery, fine dining. All units are spacious and nicely decorated, many with views of the Strip and fountains. 36 stories; interior corridors. **Rooms:** 3005. Some shower baths, some whirlpools, safes, ⊘. 🔲, roll-in showers, 🔲. **Recreation:** Pools, whirlpools, massage, game room. **Services:** Valet parking, area transportation, laundry, business services. **Dining:** 6 dining rooms, 4 restaurants (see listings for Olives at Bellagio, Picasso and Prime Steakhouse); coffee shop; 2 delis; buffet; $11-85; cocktails.

BEST INN & SUITES 🏧

♦♦♦ Motel

(702) 632-0229 Rates not provided
I-15 exit Craig, E to N Las Vegas Bl; 4288 N Nellis Bl.
Continental breakfast. AE, CB, DI, DS, MC, VI. Pets, $10 extra charge. 3 stories; interior corridors. **Rooms:** 59. Some shower baths, some whirlpools, ⊘. Roll-in showers, 🔲. **Recreation:** Whirlpool. **Services:** Laundry, business services.

BEST WESTERN MAIN STREET INN 🏧

♦♦ Motor Inn

(702) 382-3455 $39-149
I-15 exit 43E northbound, 44E southbound; 1000 N Main St.
XP $7. AE, CB, DI, DS, MC, VI. Small pets only, $8 extra charge. 2-3 stories; exterior corridors. **Rooms:** 91. ⊘ **Recreation:** Pools. **Services:** Laundry, business services. **Dining:** Restaurant; $7-12; 6 am-11 pm.

BEST WESTERN MARDI GRAS INN 🏧

♦♦ Motor Inn

(702) 731-2020 Rates not provided
½ mi S of convention center; 3500 Paradise Rd.
Continental breakfast. AE, CB, DI, DS, MC, VI. Gift shop, video tape library. 3 stories; exterior corridors. **Rooms:** 314. Video games, ⊘. 🔲 **Recreation:** Pools, whirlpool, sun deck. **Services:** Area transportation, laundry, business services. **Dining:** Restaurant; $9-14; 24 hrs; cocktails.

BEST WESTERN MCCARRAN INN 🏧

♦♦ Motel

(702) 798-5530 Rates not provided
I-15 exit Tropicana, E 5½ blks to Paradise Rd; 4970 Paradise Rd.

Continental breakfast. AE, CB, DI, DS, MC, VI. 3 stories; interior corridors. ☒ **Rooms:** 100. ⊘ **Recreation:** Pools. **Services:** Area transportation, laundry.

BEST WESTERN NELLIS MOTOR INN ⑭   ♦♦ Motel
(702) 643-6111   Rates not provided
I-15 exit 48 eastbound, 7 mi NE; ⅓ mi from Nellis AFB; 5330 E Craig Rd.
Continental breakfast. AE, CB, DI, DS, MC, VI. Pets, $10 extra charge. 2 stories; exterior corridors. **Rooms:** 52. ⊘ **Recreation:** Pools, playground. **Services:** Laundry.

BEST WESTERN PARKVIEW INN ⑭   ♦♦ Motel
(702) 385-1213 $39-149
I-15 exit US 93-95; ⅓ mi N at Washington; 921 Las Vegas Bl N.
XP $7. Continental breakfast. 7-day refund notice. AE, CB, DI, DS, MC, VI. Small pets only, $8 extra charge. 2 stories; exterior corridors. **Rooms:** 42. ⊘ **Recreation:** Pools. **Services:** Laundry.

BOARDWALK CASINO-HOLIDAY INN ⑭   ♦♦♦ Hotel
(702) 735-2400 $49-179
I-15 exit Flamingo Bl, S on Strip; 3750 Las Vegas Bl S.
XP $15. AE, CB, DI, DS, MC, VI. Gift shop. 4-16 stories; interior/exterior corridors. Roll-in showers, ☒. **Rooms:** 654. Some shower baths, some whirlpools, ⊘. **Recreation:** Pools, exercise room. **Services:** Valet parking, laundry, business services. **Dining:** Restaurant; deli; buffet; $9-25; cocktails.

BOULDER PALMS LUXURY SUITES ⑭   ♦♦ Suite Motel
(702) 434-9900   Rates not provided
I-15 exit E Flamingo; 6 mi E to Boulder, then N; 4350 Boulder Hwy.
AE, CB, DI, DS, MC, VI. 2 stories; exterior corridors. **Rooms:** 182. Some shower baths, kitchens, ⊘. **Recreation:** Pools, whirlpool, exercise room. **Services:** Area transportation, laundry, business services.

BOULDER STATION HOTEL CASINO ⑭   ♦♦♦ Hotel
(702) 432-7777   Rates not provided
4111 Boulder Hwy.
AE, CB, DI, DS, MC, VI. Gift shop. Casino, movie theater. 13 stories; interior corridors. **Rooms:** 300. Some shower baths, some whirlpools, ⊘. Roll-in showers. **Recreation:** Pools. **Services:** Valet parking, laundry, business services. **Dining:** 2 dining rooms (see listing for Pasta Palace); 2 restaurants; coffee shop; buffet; $10-20; cocktails.

CAESARS PALACE   ♦♦♦♦ Hotel
(702) 731-7110   Rates not provided
I-15 exit E Flamingo Rd; 4½ mi S, on the Strip; 3570 Las Vegas Bl S.
AE, CB, DI, DS, MC, VI. Gift shop. Elegant shops, art galleries. Attractively landscaped grounds and marble statuary. The Forum Mall resembles a Roman streetscape. 14-29 stories; interior corridors. **Rooms:** 2454. Some shower baths, some whirlpools, safes, ⊘. 🖳, roll-in showers, ☒. **Recreation:** Pools, sauna, whirlpools, massage. **Services:** Valet parking, laundry, business services. **Dining:** See listing for Neros Steak and Seafood.

CANDLEWOOD SUITES   ♦♦♦ Extended Stay Motel
(702) 836-3660   Rates not provided
I-15 exit E Flamingo Rd; E to Paradise Rd, just NE; 4034 S Paradise Rd.

AE, CB, DI, DS, MC, VI. Gift shop. 4 stories; interior corridors. **Rooms:** 276. Some shower baths, CD players, ⊘. Roll-in showers. **Recreation:** Pools, whirlpool, exercise room. **Services:** Laundry, business services.

CARRIAGE HOUSE ⏺   ♦♦♦ Hotel
(702) 798-1020 $145-300
Just E off the Strip; 105 E Harmon Av.
AE, CB, DI, DS, MC, VI. 9 stories; interior corridors. **Rooms:** 140. Some shower baths, some kitchens and efficiencies, video games, safes, ⊘. Roll-in showers. **Recreation:** Pools, whirlpool, lighted tennis court. **Services:** Laundry, business services.

CASINO ROYALE AND HOTEL   ♦♦ Motel
(702) 737-3500 $39-99
Center of the Strip; 3411 Las Vegas Bl S.
XP $10. AE, MC, VI. 4 stories; interior corridors. **Rooms:** 153. Safes, ⊘. **Recreation:** Pools. **Services:** Laundry.

CIRCUS CIRCUS HOTEL, CASINO & THEMEPARK   ♦♦♦ Hotel
(702) 734-0410   Rates not provided
2¾ mi S on the Strip; 2880 Las Vegas Bl S.
AE, CB, DI, DS, MC, VI. Gift shop. 2-35 stories; interior corridors. **Rooms:** 3770. Some shower baths, some whirlpools, safes, ⊘, 🖳, roll-in showers, 🖳. **Recreation:** Pools, whirlpools. **Services:** Valet parking, laundry, business services. **Dining:** See listing for Blue Iguana.

COMFORT INN ⏺   ♦♦♦ Motel
(702) 399-1500 $59-250
I-15 exit 46 (Cheyenne W); 910 E Cheyenne Av.
XP $10. Continental breakfast. AE, CB, DI, DS, MC, VI. Pets, $5 extra charge. Gift shop. 3 stories, interior corridors. **Rooms:** 59. Some shower baths, some whirlpools, ⊘. Roll-in showers. **Recreation:** Pools, whirlpool. **Services:** Laundry, business services.

COMFORT INN SOUTH ⏺   ♦♦ Motel
(702) 736-3600   Rates not provided
I-15 exit Tropicana Av, ½ mi E; 5075 S Koval Ln.
Continental breakfast. AE, CB, DI, DS, MC, VI. 2 stories; exterior corridors. **Rooms:** 106. ⊘ **Recreation:** Pools. **Services:** Laundry.

COURTYARD BY MARRIOTT-CONVENTION CENTER ⏺   ♦♦♦ Motor Inn
(702) 791-3600   Rates not provided
Just E of Strip; 1 blk to convention center; 3275 Paradise Rd.
AE, CB, DI, DS, MC, VI. 3 stories; interior corridors. **Rooms:** 149. ⊘ 🖳 **Recreation:** Pools, whirlpool, exercise room. **Services:** Laundry, business services.

COURTYARD BY MARRIOTT LAS VEGAS-SUMMERLIN ⏺   ♦♦♦ Motel
(702) 646-4400   Rates not provided
US 95 exit Lake Mead Bl E; 1901 N Rainbow Bl.
AE, CB, DI, DS, MC, VI. 3 stories; interior corridors. **Rooms:** 154. Some shower baths, some whirlpools, ⊘. Roll-in showers. **Recreation:** Pools, whirlpool, exercise room. **Services:** Laundry, business services.

CROWNE PLAZA 🆀   ♦♦♦ Motor Inn
(702) 369-4400 $89-185
I-15 exit E Flamingo Rd; ½ mi E to Paradise Rd, ⅓ mi S; 4255 S Paradise Rd.
XP $20. 3-day refund notice; cancellation fee. AE, CB, DI, DS, MC, VI. Pets; $200 deposit; restricted to first floor. Gift shop. **Rooms:** 201. Video games, ∅. 🖱, 🗗. **Recreation:** Pools, sauna, whirlpool, exercise room. **Services:** Valet parking, area transportation, laundry, business services. **Dining:** Restaurant; $8-16; 6 am-10 pm; cocktails.

DAYS INN DOWNTOWN   ♦♦ Motel
(702) 388-1400   Rates not provided
On US 93/95 business route; 707 E Fremont St.
AE, CB, DI, DS, MC, VI. 3 stories; exterior corridors. **Rooms:** 147. ∅ 🗗 **Recreation:** Pools.

DAYS INN-TOWN HALL CASINO 🆀   ♦ Motel
(702) 731-2111 $45-125
Just E off the Strip, near Flamingo ; 4155 Koval Ln.
XP $6. Cancellation fee. AE, CB, DI, DS, MC, VI. Gift shop. 3 stories; interior corridors. **Rooms:** 357. Some shower baths, safes, ∅. **Recreation:** Pools, whirlpool. **Services:** Laundry. **Dining:** Coffee shop; $5-10; 24 hrs.

DESERT PARADISE RESORT 🆀   ♦♦♦ Motel
(702) 257-0010 $99-399
I-15 exit Tropicana Av W, then S; 5165 S Decatur Bl.
AE, CB, DI, DS, MC, VI. 2 stories; exterior corridors. **Rooms:** 152. Some kitchens, ∅. **Recreation:** Pools, whirlpools, exercise room, massage. **Services:** Area transportation, laundry, business services.

DOUBLETREE CLUB HOTEL LAS VEGAS AIRPORT 🆀   ♦♦♦ Hotel
(702) 948-4000 $69-209
I-215 exit 7 (Warm Springs Rd); 7250 Pollock Dr.
XP $10. AE, CB, DI, DS, MC, VI. 6 stories; interior corridors. **Rooms:** 190. Some shower baths, video games, ∅. Roll-in showers, 🗗. **Recreation:** Exercise room. **Services:** Valet parking, laundry, business services.

ECONO LODGE 🆀   ♦ Motel
(702) 382-6001 $35-209
I-15 exit E Charleston, to Las Vegas Bl, then S; 1150 Las Vegas Bl S.
7-day refund notice. AE, CB, DI, DS, MC, VI. 2 stories; exterior corridors. **Rooms:** 123. ∅ **Recreation:** Pools.

ECONO LODGE BY THE STRIP   ♦♦ Motel
(702) 733-7800   Rates not provided
I-15 exit E Flamingo Rd, at Koval Rd; 211 E Flamingo Rd.
AE, CB, DI, DS, MC, VI. 2 stories; exterior corridors. **Rooms:** 121.

EMBASSY SUITES CONVENTION CENTER 🆀   ♦♦♦ Suite Motor Inn
(702) 893-8000 $99-199
I-15 exit Sahara E; ½ mi S of convention center; 3600 Paradise Rd.
XP $10. AE, CB, DI, DS, MC, VI. Gift shop. 11 stories; interior corridors. **Rooms:** 286. Some shower baths, extended cable TV, high-speed Internet, video games, ∅. **Recreation:** Pools, whirlpool, exercise room. **Services:** Laundry, business services.

EMBASSY SUITES HOTEL LAS VEGAS
♦♦♦ Hotel
(702) 795-2800   Rates not provided
I-15 E on Tropicana Ln, then N; 4315 Swenson Av.
AE, CB, DI, DS, MC, VI. Gift shop. 6 stories; interior corridors. **Rooms:** 220. Some shower baths, extended cable TV, ⊘. **Recreation:** Pools, whirlpools, exercise room. **Services:** Laundry, business services.

EMERALD SPRINGS-HOLIDAY INN
♦♦♦ Motor Inn
(702) 732-9100   Rates not provided
I-15 exit E Flamingo Rd; 325 E Flamingo Rd.
AE, CB, DI, DS, MC, VI. 3 stories; interior corridors. **Rooms:** 150. Some whirlpools, video games, ⊘. **Recreation:** Pools, whirlpool, exercise room. **Services:** Valet parking, laundry, business services.

EXCALIBUR HOTEL & CASINO
♦♦♦ Hotel
(702) 597-7777   Rates not provided
I-15 exit E Tropicana Av; 3850 Las Vegas Bl S.
AE, DI, DS, MC, VI. Gift shop. game room. 28 stories; interior corridors. **Rooms:** 4008. Shower baths, some whirlpools, ⊘. 🔄, roll-in showers, 🔲. **Recreation:** Whirlpool. **Services:** Valet parking, laundry, business services.

FAIRFIELD INN BY MARRIOTT ⏺
♦♦ Motel
(702) 791-0899 $49-129
I-15 exit E Flamingo Rd; 3 blks N of convention center; 3850 Paradise Rd.
Continental breakfast. AE, DI, DS, MC, VI. 4 stories; interior corridors. **Rooms:** 129. ⊘ 🔲 **Recreation:** Pools, whirlpool. **Services:** Business services.

FIESTA CASINO HOTEL
♦♦ Motor Inn
(702) 631-7000   Rates not provided
3 mi N of downtown; 2400 N Rancho Dr.
AE, DI, DS, MC, VI. Gift shop. 5 stories; interior corridors. **Rooms:** 100. Some shower baths, ⊘. Roll-in showers. **Recreation:** Pools. **Services:** Valet parking, business services.

FITZGERALDS CASINO & HOLIDAY INN
♦♦♦ Hotel
(702) 388-2400   Rates not provided
In downtown casino center; 301 Fremont St.
AE, CB, DI, DS, MC, VI. Gift shop. 34 stories; interior corridors. **Rooms:** 640. Some whirlpools, safes, ⊘. **Services:** Valet parking, business services.

FLAMINGO LAS VEGAS ⏺
♦♦♦ Hotel
(Formerly the Flamingo Las Vegas)
(702) 733-3111   Rates not provided
I-15 exit Flamingo Rd E, N on the Strip; 3555 Las Vegas Bl S.
AE, CB, DI, DS, MC, VI. Gift shop. 2-28 stories; interior corridors. **Rooms:** 3638. Some shower baths, safes, ⊘. Roll-in showers, 🔲. **Recreation:** Pools, waterslide, saunas, whirlpools, massage, 4 lighted tennis courts, sports court. **Services:** Valet parking, laundry, business services. **Dining:** 5 Restaurants; coffee shop; $7-30; 24 hrs; cocktails.

FOUR SEASONS HOTEL LAS VEGAS ⏺
♦♦♦♦♦ Hotel
(702) 632-5000   Rates not provided
I-15 exit E Tropicana, S on the Strip; 3960 Las Vegas Bl S.

AE, CB, DI, DS, MC, VI. Small pets only. Gift shop. 5 stories; interior corridors. **Rooms:** 424 spacious rooms located on floors 35-39 of high-rise. Mountain views, deep soaking tubs, some shower baths, some whirlpools, high-speed Internet, safes, ⊘. Roll-in showers. **Recreation:** Pools, whirlpools, massage, jogging. **Services:** Valet parking, area transportation, laundry, business services. **Dining:** Dining room; restaurant; $20-43; cocktails; nightclub.

GOLD COAST HOTEL ⏛   ♦♦♦ Hotel
(702) 367-7111 $39-119
I-75 exit Flamingo Rd W, just W; 4000 W Flamingo Rd.
Cancellation fee. AE, CB, DI, DS, MC, VI. Gift shop, casino. 10 stories; interior corridors. **Rooms:** 711. Some shower baths, ⊘. **Recreation:** Pools, whirlpool, exercise room, bowling. **Services:** Valet parking, area transportation, laundry, business services. **Dining:** Dining room; restaurant; coffee shop; deli; $8-21; 24 hrs; cocktails.

GOLDEN NUGGET HOTEL ⏛   ♦♦♦♦ Hotel
(702) 385-7111 $59-299
Downtown, casino center area; 129 E Fremont St.
XP $20. Cancellation fee. AE, DI, DS, MC, VI. Gift shop, game room, casino. Attractive downtown property with twin towers. 10-22 stories; interior corridors. **Rooms:** 1907. Some shower baths, some whirlpools, safes, ⊘. 🔄, roll-in showers, 📶. **Recreation:** Whirlpool, massage. **Services:** Valet parking, laundry, business services. **Dining:** 2 dining rooms (see listing for Lillie Langtry's); coffee shop; deli; buffet; 24 hrs; $7-35; cocktails.

HAMPTON INN TROPICANA   ♦♦♦ Motel
(702) 948-8100   Rates not provided
I-15 exit W Tropicana; 4975 S Industrial Rd.
AE, CB, DI, DS, MC, VI. Gift shop. 6 stories; interior corridors. **Rooms:** 320. Some shower baths, video games, ⊘. Roll-in showers. **Recreation:** Pools, whirlpool, exercise room. **Services:** Laundry, business services.

HARRAH'S-LAS VEGAS   ♦♦♦ Hotel
(702) 369-5000   Rates not provided
I-15 exit E Flamingo; 3475 Las Vegas Bl S.
XP $15. Gift shop. 15-35 stories; interior corridors. **Rooms:** 2601. Some shower baths, some whirlpools, video games, ⊘. 🔄, roll-in showers, 📶. **Recreation:** Pools, saunas, whirlpools, steam rooms, massage. **Services:** Valet parking, laundry, business services. **Dining:** See listing for Range Steakhouse at Harrah's.

HAWTHORN INN & SUITES ⏛   ♦♦♦ Motel
(702) 798-7736   Rates not provided
I-15 exit 37, Tropicana Av W; 4975 S Valley View Bl.
Continental breakfast. AE, CB, DI, DS, MC. Pets, $18 fee. Gift shop. 3 stories, interior corridors. **Rooms:** 59. Some shower baths, some kitchens, ⊘. Roll-in showers. **Recreation:** Pools, whirlpool, exercise room. **Services:** Laundry.

HAWTHORN SUITES-LAS VEGAS   ♦♦♦ Suite Motel
(702) 739-7000 $120-210
I-15 exit E Tropicana Av; ¼ mi E to Duke Ellington Wy, just S; 5051 Duke Ellington Wy.
Cancellation fee. AE, CB, DI, DS, MC, VI. Small pets only, $125 fee. Gift shop. 3 stories; exterior corridors. **Rooms:** 278. Some shower baths, high-speed Internet, video

games, ⊘. Roll-in showers, ▣. **Recreation:** Pools, whirlpool, exercise room, sports court. **Services:** Laundry, business services.

HAWTHORN SUITES LTD ⏺   ♦♦♦ Motel
(702) 243-0356   Rates not provided
Just W of Fort Apache; 9570 W Sahara.
Continental breakfast. AE, CB, DI, DS, MC, VI. Small pets only, $25 fee. 3 stories; interior corridors. **Rooms:** 75. Some shower baths, some whirlpools, ⊘. Roll-in showers. **Recreation:** Pools, whirlpool, exercise room. **Services:** Laundry, business services.

HILTON GRAND VACATIONS CLUB   ♦♦♦ Extended Stay Hotel
(702) 697-2900 $129-449
I-15 exit E Flamingo Rd, N on the Strip; directly behind Flamingo Las Vegas; 3575 Las Vegas Bl S.
3-day refund notice. AE, DI, DS, MC, VI. Gift shop. 17 stories; interior corridors. **Rooms:** 303. Some whirlpools, some efficiencies or kitchens, ⊘. Roll-in showers, ▣. **Recreation:** Pools, sauna, whirlpools, exercise room. **Services:** Valet parking, laundry.

HILTON GRAND VACATIONS CLUB AT THE LAS VEGAS HILTON ⏺
        ♦♦♦ Hotel
(702) 946-9200 $129-449
At Paradise Rd adj to Las Vegas Hilton; 455 Karen Av.
AE, DI, DS, MC, VI. Gift shop. 16 stories; interior corridors. **Rooms:** 405. Some shower baths, some whirlpools, safes, ⊘. **Recreation:** Pools, whirlpools, exercise room, jogging. **Services:** Laundry.

HOLIDAY INN EXPRESS ⏺   ♦♦♦ Motel
(702) 256-3766   Rates not provided
I-15 exit Sahara Av, 6½ mi W; 8669 W Sahara Av.
Continental breakfast. AE, CB, DI, DS, MC, VI. Gift shop. Pets, $20 fee; in smoking units. 3 stories; interior corridors. **Rooms:** 59. Some shower baths, some whirlpools, ⊘. Roll-in showers. **Recreation:** Pools, whirlpool. **Services:** Laundry, business services.

HOLIDAY INN EXPRESS HOTEL & SUITES N LAS VEGAS   ♦♦♦ Motel
(702) 649-3000   Rates not provided
I-15 exit W Craig Rd; 4540 Donovan Wy.
AE, CB, DI, DS, MC, VI. Pets, $25 fee. Gift shop. 3 stories; interior corridors. **Rooms:** 74. Some shower baths, some whirlpools, ⊘. Roll-in showers. **Recreation:** Pools, whirlpool. **Services:** Laundry, business services.

HOWARD JOHNSON HOTEL & CASINO   ♦♦ Hotel
(702) 798-1111 $49-199
I-15 exit W Tropicana Av; 3111 W Tropicana Av.
XP $10. Cancellation fee. AE, DI, DS, MC, VI. 6 stories; interior corridors. **Rooms:** 150. ⊘ **Recreation:** Pools, whirlpool. **Services:** Laundry, business services.

HOWARD JOHNSON INN-AIRPORT   ♦ Motel
(702) 798-2777 $40-150
I-15 exit E Tropicana Av; 1¾ mi to Paradise Rd, ⅓ mi S; 5100 Paradise Rd.
Cancellation fee. AE, CB, DI, DS, MC, VI. Gift shop. 2 stories; exterior corridors. **Rooms:** 327. ⊘ Roll-in showers, ▣. **Recreation:** Pools, exercise room. **Services:** Laundry, business services.

HOWARD JOHNSON LAS VEGAS STRIP ⍟   ♦♦ Motor Inn
(702) 388-0301 $39-89
I-15 exit Sahara E, to Las Vegas Bl, then N; 1401 Las Vegas Bl S.
XP $10. Small pets only, $10 extra charge. 3 stories; interior/exterior corridors.
Rooms: 104. Some whirlpools, safes, ⊘. **Recreation:** Pools. **Services:** Laundry, business services.

KEY LARGO CASINO & HOTEL ⍟   ♦♦ Hotel
(702) 733-7777 $39-99
I-15 exit 38, at E Flamingo Rd, 4 blks to 377 E Flamingo Rd.
AE, CB, DI, DS, MC, VI. Gift shop. 3 stories; interior/exterior corridors. **Rooms:** 316.
⊘ ▣ **Recreation:** Pools, whirlpool. **Services:** Laundry, business services.

KOALA MOTEL & APARTMENTS ⍟   ♦ Motel
(702) 384-8211   Rates not provided
I-15 exit downtown casino center; 520 S Casino Center Bl.
AE, CB, DI, DS, MC, VI. 3 stories; interior corridors. **Rooms:** 48. ⊘ **Services:** Laundry.

LA QUINTA INN ⍟   ♦♦♦ Motel
(702) 739-7457   Rates not provided
5½ mi S on the Strip; 3782 Las Vegas Bl S.
Continental breakfast. AE, CB, DI, DS, MC, VI. Small pets only. 3 stories; exterior corridors. **Rooms:** 114. Video games, ⊘. **Recreation:** Pools.

LA QUINTA INN CONVENTION CENTER ⍟   ♦♦♦ Motel
(702) 796-9000   Rates not provided
I-15 exit E Flamingo Rd; ¾ mi S of convention center, ½ mi E of the Strip; 3970 Paradise Rd.
Continental breakfast. AE, CB, DI, DS, MC, VI. 3 stories; interior corridors. **Rooms:** 251. Some shower baths, some whirlpools, video games, ⊘. Roll-in showers. **Recreation:** Pools, whirlpool, exercise room. **Services:** Area transportation, laundry, business services.

LA QUINTA LAS VEGAS NW TECH CENTER   ♦♦♦ Motel
(702) 360-1200   Rates not provided
I-95 exit 83, on W Cheyenne Av; 7101 Cascade Valley Ct.
AE, CB, DI, DS, MC, VI. 5 stories; interior corridors. **Rooms:** 128. Some shower baths, ⊘. **Recreation:** Pools, whirlpool, exercise room. **Services:** Laundry, business services.

LAS VEGAS HILTON ⍟   ♦♦♦♦ Hotel
(702) 732-5111   Rates not provided
I-15 exit Sahara, 2 mi E; adj to convention center; 3000 Paradise Rd.
AE, CB, DI, DS, MC, VI. Gift shop, game room, Star Trek experience. 30 stories; interior corridors. **Rooms:** 3174. Some shower baths, some whirlpools, safes, ⊘. ⍟, roll-in showers, ▣. **Recreation:** Whirlpools, massage, 6 lighted tennis courts. **Services:** Valet parking, laundry, business services. **Dining:** 8 dining rms (see listings for Andiamo and Hilton Steakhouse); coffee shop; buffet; $7-50; 24 hrs; cocktails.

LUXOR LAS VEGAS   ♦♦♦ Hotel
(702) 262-4000   Rates not provided
I-15 exit E Tropicana Av, just S on the Strip; 3900 Las Vegas Bl S.
AE, CB, DI, DS, MC, VI. Gift shop. 30 stories; interior corridors. **Rooms:** 4407. Some shower baths, some whirlpools, ⊘. ⍟, roll-in showers, ▣. **Recreation:** Pools, saunas,

whirlpools, massage. **Services:** Valet parking, laundry, business services. **Dining:** See listing for Sacred Sea Room.

MAIN STREET STATION
(702) 387-1896
In downtown casino center; 200 N Main St.
◆◆◆ Hotel
Rates not provided

AE, CB, DI, DS, MC, VI. Gift shop. 17 stories; interior corridors. **Rooms:** 406. Some shower baths, video games, safes, ⌀. Roll-in showers. **Services:** Valet parking, business services.

MANDALAY BAY RESORT & CASINO 🆎
(702) 632-7777
I-15 exit E Tropicana, just E; 3950 Las Vegas Bl S.
◆◆◆◆ Resort
Rates not provided

AE, CB, DI, DS, MC, VI. Spacious, elegant, fun and distinctive units. Gift shop, spa, casino and shops. 42 stories; interior corridors. **Rooms:** 3220. Some shower baths, some whirlpools, safes, ⌀. Roll-in showers. **Recreation:** Pools, whirlpools, massage, jogging. **Services:** Valet parking, area transportation, laundry, business services. **Dining:** 6 dining rms, 10 restaurants (see listings for Aureole, Border Grill and 3950 Restaurant); coffee shop; deli; buffet; $10-50; 24 hrs; cocktails.

MARRIOTT SUITES LAS VEGAS 🆎
(702) 650-2000
Near convention center; at Paradise Rd; 325 Convention Center Dr.
◆◆◆ Hotel
$129-389

AE, CB, DI, DS, MC, VI. Gift shop. 17 stories; interior corridors. **Rooms:** 278. Some shower baths, high-speed Internet. **Recreation:** Pools, whirlpool, exercise room. **Services:** Laundry, business services. **Dining:** Restaurant; $12-21; 6:30 am-11 pm.

MGM GRAND HOTEL AND CASINO
(702) 891-1111
I-15 exit Tropicana Av; 3799 Las Vegas Bl S.
◆◆◆ Hotel
Rates not provided

AE, CB, DI, DS, MC, VI. Gift shop. 30 stories; interior corridors. **Rooms:** 5005. Some shower baths, some whirlpools, safes, ⌀. 🔲, roll-in showers, 🔲. **Recreation:** Pools, whirlpools, massage, game room. **Services:** Valet parking, laundry, business services. **Dining:** See listing for Emeril's New Orleans Fish House.

THE MIRAGE
(702) 791-7111
I-15 exit E Flamingo to Las Vegas Bl; 3400 Las Vegas Bl S.
◆◆◆◆ Hotel
Rates not provided

AE, DI, DS, MC, VI. Gift shop, game room. Lavish grounds and unique public areas, home to Siegfried and Roy's white tigers and dolphin habitat. 30 stories; interior corridors. **Rooms:** 3044. Some shower baths, some whirlpools, safes, ⌀. 🔲, roll-in showers, 🔲. **Recreation:** Pools, whirlpools, massage. **Services:** Valet parking, laundry, business services. **Dining:** See listings for Renoir and Samba Grill.

MONTE CARLO RESORT & CASINO
(702) 730-7777
On the Strip, between Flamingo Rd and Tropicana Av; 3770 Las Vegas Bl S.
◆◆◆ Hotel
$79-349

XP $15. Cancellation fee. AE, CB, DI, DS, MC, VI. Gift shop. 32 stories; interior corridors. **Rooms:** 3016. Some shower baths, some whirlpools, ⌀. Roll-in showers, 🔲. **Recreation:** Pools, sauna, whirlpool, wading pool, steam room, massage, 3 lighted tennis courts, game room. **Services:** Valet parking, laundry, business services.

THE ORLEANS ⓐⓐ
(702) 365-7111
♦♦♦ Hotel
Rates not provided

I-15 exit Tropicana Av, 1 mi W; 4500 W Tropicana Av.
AE, CB, DI, DS, MC, VI. Gift shop. Casino, movie theater. 22 stories. **Rooms:** 840. Some shower baths, some whirlpools, ⊘. Roll-in showers. **Recreation:** Pools, whirlpool, exercise room, bowling. **Services:** Valet parking, laundry, business services. **Dining:** Dining rm; 4 restaurants (see listing for Don Miguel's); coffee shop; buffet; $5-20; 24 hrs; cocktails.

PALACE STATION HOTEL & CASINO ⓐⓐ
(702) 367-2411
♦♦♦ Hotel
Rates not provided

I-15 exit Sahara Av; SW corner of Sahara Av and Rancho Rd; 2411 W Sahara Av.
AE, CB, DI, DS, MC, VI. Gift shop. 21 stories; interior corridors. **Rooms:** 1028. Some shower baths, some whirlpools, safes, ⊘. Roll-in showers, 🖅. **Recreation:** Pools, whirlpools, exercise room. **Services:** Valet parking, area transportation, laundry, business services. **Dining:** 9 restaurants; coffee shop; buffet; $12-18; 24 hrs.

PALMS CASINO HOTEL
(702) 942-7777
Nonrated Hotel
$65-409

I-15 exit W Flamingo Rd, ½ mi W; 4321 W Flamingo Rd.
Too new to rate, opening scheduled for December 2001.
XP $25. 3-day refund notice. AE, CB, DI, DS, MC, VI. **Rooms:** 447. **Recreation:** Pool. **Dining:** Restaurant.

PARIS LAS VEGAS
(702) 946-7000
♦♦♦♦ Hotel
Rates not provided

I-15 exit Flamingo E, S on the Strip; 3655 Las Vegas Bl S.
AE, CB, DI, DS, MC, VI. Gift shop. Located in the heart of the Las Vegas Strip. French-style retail shops, lounges, restaurants; Eiffel Tower. 33 stories; interior corridors. **Rooms:** 2916. Some shower baths, some whirlpools, safes, ⊘. **Recreation:** Pools, whirlpools, 8 lighted tennis courts. **Services:** Valet parking, laundry, business services. **Dining:** See listings for Eiffel Tower Restaurant and La Rotisserie des Artistes.

RAMADA INN-SPEEDWAY CASINO
(702) 399-3297
♦♦ Motor Inn
Rates not provided

I-15 exit 46 E (Cheyenne Av); 3227 Civic Center Dr.
AE, DI, DS, MC, VI. Gift shop. 3 stories; interior corridors. **Rooms:** 95. Some shower baths, ⊘. Roll-in showers. **Recreation:** Pools. **Services:** Valet parking, laundry, business services.

RAMADA VACATION SUITES
(702) 731-6100
♦♦♦ Extended Stay Motel
Rates not provided

I-15 exit E Flamingo Rd to Audrie, then just N; 100 Winnick Av.
AE, DI, DS, MC, VI. Gift shop. 3 stories; interior/exterior corridors. **Rooms:** 489. Some shower baths, some whirlpools, safes, ⊘. Roll-in showers, 🖅. **Recreation:** Pools, saunas, whirlpools, exercise room. **Services:** Laundry.

RESIDENCE INN-HUGHES CENTER
(702) 650-0040
♦♦♦ Motel

I-15 exit Flamingo E, at Paradise Rd; 370 Hughes Center Dr.
AE, CB, DI, DS, MC, VI. Pets, $50 fee. 11 stories; interior corridors. **Rooms:** 256. Some

shower baths, some kitchens. **Recreation:** Pools, whirlpool, exercise room. **Services:** Laundry.

RESIDENCE INN LAS VEGAS CONVENTION CENTER ⒶⒶ   ♦♦♦ Hotel
(702) 796-9300   Rates not provided
Opposite convention center; 3225 Paradise Rd.
AE, CB, DI, DS, MC, VI. Small pets only, $10 extra charge, $50 fee. 2 stories; exterior corridors. **Rooms:** 192. Some kitchens, some shower baths, ⊘. **Recreation:** Pools, whirlpools, sports court. **Services:** Laundry, business services.

RIO SUITE HOTEL & CASINO   ♦♦♦ Hotel
(702) 252-7777   Rates not provided
I-15 exit Flamingo Rd, 1/3 mi W; 3700 W Flamingo Rd.
AE, CB, DI, DS, MC, VI. Gift shop, game room. 41 stories; interior corridors. **Rooms:** 2548. Some shower baths, some whirlpools, safes, high-speed Internet, ⊘. 🖫, roll-in showers, 🖵. **Recreation:** Pools, whirlpools, massage, golf. **Services:** Valet parking, laundry, business services.

RIVIERA HOTEL AND CASINO   ♦♦♦ Hotel
(702) 734-5110   Rates not provided
I-15 exit E Sahara; 2901 Las Vegas Bl S.
AE, CB, DI, DS, MC, VI. Gift shop. 24 stories; interior corridors. **Rooms:** 2073. Some shower baths, some whirlpools, safes, ⊘. Roll-in showers, 🖵. **Recreation:** Pools, 2 lighted tennis courts, massage. **Services:** Valet parking, laundry, business services.

ST TROPEZ ALL SUITE HOTEL ⒶⒶ   ♦♦♦ Complex
(702) 369-5400   Rates not provided
2 mi S of convention center, at Paradise Rd; 455 E Harmon Av.
AE, DI, DS, MC, VI. 2 stories; interior/exterior corridors. **Rooms:** 149. Some shower baths, some whirlpools, safes. Roll-in showers, 🖵. **Recreation:** Pools, whirlpool, exercise room. **Services:** Area transportation, laundry, business services.

SAM'S TOWN HOTEL & GAMBLING HALL ⒶⒶ   ♦♦♦ Hotel
(702) 456-7777   Rates not provided
1 mi E of I-515/SR 93 and 95, Flamingo exit; 5111 Boulder Hwy.
AE, CB, DI, DS, MC, VI. Gift shop, casino, movie complex. 9 stories; interior corridors. **Rooms:** 646. Some shower baths, some whirlpools, ⊘. Roll-in showers, 🖵. **Recreation:** Pools, whirlpool, game room, bowling. **Services:** Valet parking, area transportation, laundry, business services. **Dining:** 6 restaurants (see listing for Billy Bob's Steak House & Saloon); coffee shop; deli; buffet; $6-24; cocktails.

SILVERTON HOTEL-CASINO   ♦♦ Hotel
(702) 263-7777   Rates not provided
I-15 exit 33 (W Blue Diamond Rd); 3333 Blue Diamond Rd.
AE, CB, DI, DS, MC, VI. Gift shop. 4 stories; interior corridors. **Rooms:** 304. Some shower baths, whirlpools, ⊘. Roll-in showers, 🖵. **Recreation:** Pools, whirlpool. **Services:** Valet parking, laundry, business services.

SOMERSET HOUSE MOTEL ⒶⒶ   ♦♦ Motel
(702) 735-4411   Rates not provided
3 mi S, just E off the Strip; 1 blk W from convention center; 294 Convention Center Dr.

AE, CB, DI, MC, VI. 3 stories; interior/exterior corridors. **Rooms:** 104. Some shower baths, ⊘. 🖢, roll-in showers. **Recreation:** Pools. **Services:** Laundry, business services.

STRATOSPHERE   ♦♦♦ Hotel
(702) 380-7777   Rates not provided
Just N of Sahara; 2000 Las Vegas Bl S.
AE, CB, DI, DS, MC, VI. Gift shop. 24 stories; interior corridors. **Rooms:** 2444. Some shower baths, some whirlpools, safes, ⊘. **Recreation:** Pools, whirlpool, exercise room. **Services:** Valet parking, laundry, business services.

SUNCOAST HOTEL & CASINO   ♦♦♦ Hotel
(702) 636-7111 $59-139
I-95 exit Summerlin Pkwy, to Rampart; 9090 Alta Dr.
XP $10. Cancellation fee. AE, DI, DS, MC, VI. Gift shop. 10 stories; interior corridors. **Rooms:** 432. Some shower baths, some whirlpools. **Recreation:** Pools, whirlpool, exercise room, game room. **Services:** Valet parking, business services. **Dining:** See listing for Primo's – A Place for Steaks.

SUPER 8 MOTEL-BOULDER HWY 🆀   ♦♦ Motel
(702) 435-8888 $40-128
At Harmon; 5288 Boulder Hwy.
XP $5. Cancellation fee. AE, CB, DI, DS, MC, VI. Gift shop. 4 stories; interior corridors. **Rooms:** 150. ⊘ **Recreation:** Pools, whirlpool, exercise room. **Services:** Laundry. **Dining:** Coffee shop; $6-10; 24 hrs.

SUPER 8 MOTEL LAS VEGAS STRIP   ♦♦ Motor Inn
(702) 794-0888   Rates not provided
I-15 exit Flamingo Rd E, exit S Koval; 4250 S Koval Ln.
2-night minimum stay. AE, CB, DI, DS, MC, VI. Small pets only, $8 extra charge; in smoking units. 3 stories; interior corridors. **Rooms:** 288. Some shower baths, ⊘. Roll-in showers, 🗓. **Recreation:** Pools, whirlpool. **Services:** Laundry, business services.

TEXAS STATION GAMBLING HALL & HOTEL 🆀   ♦♦♦ Hotel
(702) 631-1000   Rates not provided
Business US 95; 3 mi N of downtown; 2101 Texas Star Ln.
AE, CB, DI, DS, MC, VI. Gift shop, casino, 18-screen movie theater, wedding chapel. 6 stories; interior corridors. **Rooms:** 200. Safes, ⊘. **Recreation:** Pools, bowling, game room. **Services:** Valet parking, laundry, business services. **Dining:** 2 dining rooms; restaurant (see listing for Austins); coffee shop; buffet; $4-25; 24 hrs.

THRIFTLODGE 🆀   ♦ Motel
(702) 643-9220   Rates not provided
I-15 exit Craig Rd W; 1½ mi to Las Vegas Bl, then S; 4244 Las Vegas Bl.
Continental breakfast. AE, CB, DI, DS, MC, VI. Pets, $60 fee. 2 stories; exterior corridors. **Rooms:** 36. Some kitchens, ⊘. **Services:** Laundry.

TRAVELODGE LAS VEGAS STRIP   ♦ Motel
(702) 735-4222   Rates not provided
I-15 exit Sahara E; 2830 Las Vegas Bl S.

AE, CB, DI, DS, MC, VI. 2 stories; exterior corridors. **Rooms:** 100. Some shower baths, safes. **Recreation:** Pools.

TRAVELODGE-WEST SAHARA ♦♦ Motel
(702) 733-0001 Rates not provided
I-15 E exit 42, just W of the Strip; I-15 W, Sahara traffic exit, right via Western Av; 1501 W Sahara Av.
AE, DI, DS, MC, VI. 3-4 stories; interior corridors. **Rooms:** 223. ⊘ Roll-in showers. **Recreation:** Pools. **Services:** Laundry, business services.

TREASURE ISLAND AT THE MIRAGE ⒶⒶ ♦♦♦♦ Hotel
(702) 894-7444 $69-359
3½ mi S on the Strip; 3300 Las Vegas Bl S.
XP $25. AE, CB, DI, DS, MC, VI. Gift shop. Wide selection of dining, retail and entertainment. Comfortable units with great views of Vegas Strip and mountains. 36 stories; interior corridors. **Rooms:** 2885. Some shower baths, some whirlpools, some high-speed Internet. ⑤, roll-in showers, ☒. **Recreation:** Pools, whirlpool, massage. **Services:** Valet parking, area transportation, laundry, business services. **Dining:** 3 dining rms, 3 restaurants (see listings for Buccaneer Bay Club and Francesco's); coffee shop; deli; theme buffet; $7-15; 24 hrs; cocktails.

TROPICANA RESORT AND CASINO ♦♦ Hotel
(702) 739-2222 $59-329
I-15 exit Tropicana E; 3801 Las Vegas Bl S.
XP $20. Cancellation fee. AE, CB, DI, DS, MC, VI. Gift shop. 3-22 stories; interior corridors. **Rooms:** 1878. Some shower baths, some whirlpools, safes. **Recreation:** Pools, saunas, whirlpools, massage. **Services:** Valet parking, laundry, business services.

THE VENETIAN RESORT HOTEL CASINO ♦♦♦♦ Hotel
(702) 414-1000 $129-999
On the Strip; 3355 Las Vegas Bl S.
XP $35. 3-day refund notice; cancellation fee. AE, CB, DI, DS, MC, VI. Gift shop. Large exquisite lobby with attractive artwork and marble. Wide selection of restaurants and extensive retail shops. Very attractive Strip property featuring large comfortable units, many with views. 36 stories; interior corridors. **Rooms:** 3036. Some shower baths, some whirlpools, safes, ⊘. **Recreation:** Pools, whirlpools, massage. **Services:** Valet parking, laundry, business services. **Dining:** See listings for Delmonico Steakhouse and Lutece.

WELLESLEY INN & SUITES ⒶⒶ ♦♦♦ Extended Stay Motel
(702) 731-3111 $49-149
I-15 exit E Flamingo Rd, then 2 mi; 1550 E Flamingo Rd.
XP $10. Continental breakfast. 2-night minimum stay. AE, CB, DI, DS, MC, VI. 3 stories; interior corridors. **Rooms:** 125. Some shower baths, video games, ⊘. Roll-in showers, ☒. **Recreation:** Pools, exercise room. **Services:** Laundry, business services.

Restaurants

AL DENTE ♦♦♦ Italian
(702) 967-4656 Dinner $14-33
On the Strip; in Bally's Las Vegas, 3645 Las Vegas Bl S.
Open 6-11 pm. Closed Tue-Wed. AE, CB, MC, VI. Casual dress. Attentive service makes

for a pleasant dining experience. ⊘ Cocktails & lounge. **Reservations:** Suggested. **Services:** On-site and valet parking. **Menu:** Extensive selection of Italian dishes, set in a bustling atmosphere. A la carte.

ANDIAMO ♦♦♦ Regional Italian
(702) 732-5755 Dinner $30-70
I-15 exit Sahara, 2 mi E; adj to convention center; in Las Vegas Hilton, 3000 Paradise Rd.
Open 5:30-10:30 pm. AE, CB, DC, DS, MC, VI. Casual dress. Comfortable and elegant surroundings, nice variety of dishes. ⊘ Cocktails & lounge. **Reservations:** Suggested. **Services:** On-site and valet parking. **Menu:** Italian. A la carte.

ANDRE'S FRENCH RESTAURANT ♦♦♦ French
(702) 385-5016 Dinner $26-48
At Lewis St; 401 S 6th St.
Open 6-11 pm. Closed major holidays; also Sun, 7/1-7/31. CB, DC, MC, VI. Semi-formal attire. ⊘ Cocktails & lounge; entertainment. Country-French decor; several dining rooms. **Reservations:** Suggested. **Services:** On-site and valet parking. **Menu:** A la carte.

AUREOLE ♦♦♦♦ American
(702) 632-7401 Dinner $55-75
I-15 exit E Tropicana, just E; in Mandalay Bay Resort & Casino, 3950 Las Vegas Bl.
Open 6-11 pm. AE, CB, DC, DS, MC, VI. Dressy casual. Cocktails & lounge. Classic dishes by chef Charlie Palmer makes this a favorite restaurant in fine dining circles. **Reservations:** Suggested. **Services:** On-site and valet parking. **Menu:** Prix fixe.

AUSTINS ♦♦♦ Steak House
(702) 631-1033 Dinner $25-35
3 mi N of downtown; inside Texas Station Gambling Hall & Hotel; 2101 Texas Star Ln.
Open 5-10 pm, Fri-Sat to 11 pm. AE, DC, DS, MC, VI. Dressy casual attire. ⊘ Cocktails & lounge. **Reservations:** Suggested. **Services:** On-site and valet parking. **Menu:** A la carte.

BATTISTA'S HOLE IN THE WALL ♦♦ Italian
(702) 732-1424 Dinner $20-34
I-15 exit Flamingo Rd, ⅓ mi E, 1 blk E of Strip; 4041 Audrie.
Open 4:30-10:30 pm, Fri-Sat to 11 pm. Closed Thanksgiving, 12/25. AE, CB, DC, DS, MC, VI. Casual dress. ⊘ Cocktails & lounge. Rustic. Strolling accordion player. **Reservations:** Suggested. **Services:** On-site parking. **Menu:** Dinners include house wine and cappuccino.

BILLY BOB'S STEAK HOUSE & SALOON ♦♦ Steak House
(702) 454-8031 Dinner $11-40
Boulder Hwy at E Flamingo; in Sam's Town Hotel & Gambling Hall, 5111 Boulder Hwy.
Open 5-11 pm. AE, DC, MC, VI. Casual dress. ⊘ Cocktails & lounge. Located off the atrium. Friendly staff. **Reservations:** Suggested. **Services:** On-site and valet parking. **Menu:** Large portions of steak, seafood and chicken.

BLUE IGUANA ♦♦ Mexican
(702) 734-0410 Dinner $7-13
Las Vegas Strip; inside Circus Circus Hotel, 2880 Las Vegas Bl S.
Open 5-10:30 pm, Sat to 11:30 pm. AE, CB, DC, DS, MC, VI. Casual dress. ⊘ Cocktails. Colorful decor. Friendly staff. Located on the 2nd floor near indoor theme

park. **Services:** On-site and valet parking. **Menu:** Wide selection of Mexican fare.

BORDER GRILL
♦♦♦ Mexican
(702) 632-7403 — Lunch $15-20, dinner $19-28
I-15 exit E Tropicana, just E; in Mandalay Bay Resort & Casino, 3950 Las Vegas Bl S.
Open 11:30 am-11 pm. Closed 12/25. AE, DS, MC, VI. Casual dress. ⊘ Cocktails & lounge. Indoor and outdoor seating available. Friendly staff. **Reservations:** Suggested. **Services:** On-site and valet parking. **Menu:** Authentic Mexican cuisine.

BUCCANEER BAY CLUB
♦♦♦ Continental
(702) 894-7350 — Dinner $19-36
3½ mi S on the Strip; in Treasure Island at the Mirage, 3300 Las Vegas Bl S.
Open 5-10:30 pm. AE, CB, DC, DS, MC, VI. Semi-formal attire. ⊘ Cocktails. Located on 2nd floor, overlooks pirate battles. Inviting and friendly staff. Upscale yet comfortable dining room. **Reservations:** Suggested. **Services:** On-site and valet parking. **Menu:** Contemporary continental gourmet cuisine.

CARLUCCIO'S TIVOLI GARDENS
♦♦ Italian
(702) 795-3236 — Dinner $9-16
2½ mi E of Las Vegas Bl S; at Spencer in Liberace Plaza, 1775 E Tropicana.
Open 4:30-10 pm. Closed major holidays and Mon. AE, CB, DI, DS, MC, VI. Casual dress. ⊘ Friendly staff. Popular with locals and tourists since 1984. **Services:** On-site parking. **Menu:** Extensive Italian menu.

COUNTRY INN
♦♦ American
(702) 254-0520 — Lunch $6-8, dinner $8-13
Exit I-15 Charleston, 4 mi W; S Rainbow, ⅓ mi; 1401 S Rainbow.
Open 7 am-10 pm, Fri-Sat to 11 pm. Closed 12/25. AE, DC, DS, MC, VI. Casual dress. ⊘ Beer & wine only. Attractive country decor, traditional dishes. Friendly atmosphere. **Reservations:** Suggested weekends. **Services:** On-site parking. **Menu:** A la carte, children's menu, early bird specials, carryout.

DELMONICO STEAKHOUSE
♦♦♦ Steak House
(702) 414-3737 — Lunch $16-36, dinner $21-36
On the Strip; in The Venetian Resort Hotel Casino, 3355 Las Vegas Bl S.
Open 11:30 am-2 & 5:30-10:30 pm, Fri-Sun to 11 pm. AE, DC, DS, MC, VI. Semi-formal attire. ⊘ Cocktails & lounge; entertainment. Owned by Chef Emeril Lagasse, famous for his New Orleans cooking, adds his influence to this American steakhouse. Friendly staff, modern decor. **Reservations:** Required. **Services:** On-site and valet parking. **Menu:** A la carte.

DON MIGUEL'S
♦♦ Mexican
(702) 365-7111 — Lunch $7-9, dinner $8-15
I-15 exit Tropicana Av, 1 mi W; inside the Orleans, 4500 W Tropicana Av.
Open 11 am-11 pm. AE, DC, DS, MC, VI. Casual dress. ⊘ Cocktails & lounge. Friendly staff, relaxed atmosphere. **Services:** On-site and valet parking. **Menu:** Traditional Mexican dishes.

EIFFEL TOWER RESTAURANT
♦♦♦♦ French
(702) 948-6937 — Dinner $26-69
On the Strip; in Paris Las Vegas, 3655 Las Vegas Bl S.
Open 5:30-10 pm, Sat to 10:30 pm. AE, DC, DS, MC, VI. Semi-formal attire. ⊘ Smoke-

free premises. Cocktails & lounge; entertainment. Attractively presented. Dining room overlooks Las Vegas Strip. **Reservations:** Suggested. **Services:** On-site and valet parking. **Menu:** Authentic gourmet French cuisine; a la carte.

EMERIL'S NEW ORLEANS FISH HOUSE

♦♦♦ Creole

(702) 891-7374   Lunch $18-26, dinner $19-36

On the Strip; in MGM Grand Hotel and Casino, 3799 Las Vegas Bl S.

Open 11 am-2:30 & 5:30-10:30 pm. AE, DC, DS, MC, VI. Dressy casual. ⊘ Cocktails. Presents the flavors and culture of New Orleans. Well-stocked wine selection. **Reservations:** Required. **Services:** On-site and valet parking. **Menu:** Wide selection of Creole and Cajun cooking; a la carte.

FELLINI'S ITALIAN DINING

♦♦♦ Italian

(702) 870-9999   Dinner $15-30

4 mi W of the Strip; 5555 W Charleston Bl.

Open 5-10 pm, Sat to 11 pm. Closed 12/25. AE, DS, MC, VI. Casual dress. ⊘ Cocktails & lounge; entertainment. Romantic fine dining located off the Las Vegas Strip. Soft piano music. **Reservations:** Suggested. **Services:** On-site parking. **Menu:** Wide selection of Italian specialties and desserts. A la carte.

FRANCESCO'S

♦♦♦ Italian

(702) 894-7348   Dinner $13-35

3½ mi S on the Strip; in Treasure Island at the Mirage, 3300 Las Vegas Bl S.

Open 5:30-11 pm. AE, CB, DC, DS, MC, VI. Dressy casual. ⊘ Cocktails & lounge. Features artwork from celebrities like Tony Curtis. Exhibition kitchen. **Reservations:** Suggested. **Services:** On-site and valet parking. **Menu:** Contemporary Italian cuisine.

GANDHI INDIA'S CUISINE ⒶⒶⒶ

♦♦ Indian

(702) 734-0094   Lunch $8-10, dinner $13-19

½ mi E of the Strip at Flamingo Av; 4080 Paradise Rd.

Open 11 am-2:30 & 5-10:30 pm. AE, DC, DS, MC, VI. Casual dress. ⊘ Cocktails. Popular lunch buffet favored by locals. **Reservations:** Suggested. **Services:** On-site parking. **Menu:** Authentic regional cooking of India. A la carte, buffet, children's menu.

GOLDEN STEER

♦♦ Steak House

(702) 384-4470   Dinner $20-60

I-15 exit Sahara, ⅛ mi E; 1 blk W of the Strip; 308 W Sahara Av.

Open 4:30-11 pm, Sat to 11:30 pm. Closed 12/25. AE, CB, DC, MC, VI. Dressy casual. ⊘ Cocktails & lounge. **Reservations:** Suggested. **Services:** On-site and valet parking. **Menu:** Varied, with chicken, veal and seafood entrees. Italian specialties. A la carte.

HILTON STEAKHOUSE

♦♦♦ Steak House

(702) 732-5645   Dinner $25-50

I-15 exit Sahara, 2 mi E; adjacent to convention center; in Las Vegas Hilton, 3000 Paradise Rd.

Open 5:30-10:30 pm. AE, CB, DC, DS, MC, VI. Dressy casual. Cocktails. **Reservations:** Suggested. **Services:** On-site and valet parking. **Menu:** A la carte.

LA ROTISSERIE DES ARTISTES

♦♦♦ French

(702) 967-7999   Dinner $20-33

I-15 exit Flamingo E, S on the Strip; in Paris Las Vegas, 3655 Las Vegas Bl S.

Open 5:30-11 pm. AE, CB, DC, DS, MC, VI. Casual dress. ⊘ Cocktails. An open kitchen is featured in this two-story art deco dining room. Friendly staff. **Reservations:** Suggested. **Services:** On-site and valet parking. **Menu:** Wide selection of slow-roasted fresh meats, poultry and fish. A la carte.

LAWRY'S THE PRIME RIB ♦♦♦ American
(702) 893-2223 Dinner $23-30
1 mi E of the Strip, just off Flamingo Rd; 4043 Howard Hughes Pkwy.
Open 5-10 pm, Sat-Sun to 11 pm. Closed 12/25. AE, CB, DC, DS, MC, VI. Dressy casual. Ø Cocktails & lounge. Convenient to both Las Vegas Strip and convention center. **Reservations:** Suggested. **Services:** On-site and valet parking. **Menu:** Roasted prime ribs of beef carved tableside.

LILLIE LANGTRY'S ♦♦♦ Chinese
(702) 385-7111 Dinner $10-36
Downtown; in Golden Nugget Hotel, 129 E Fremont St.
Open 5-11 pm. AE, CB, DC, DS, MC, VI. Dressy casual. Ø Cocktails. Friendly staff. Comfortable, elegant dining room. **Reservations:** Suggested. **Services:** On-site and valet parking. **Menu:** Traditional Szechuan and Cantonese cuisine, and prime mesquite-broiled steaks.

LUTECE ♦♦♦ French
(702) 414-2220 Lunch $12-34, dinner $26-40
On the Strip; in the Venetian Resort Hotel Casino, 3355 Las Vegas Bl S.
Open 11:30 am-3:30 & 5:30-11 pm. AE, DC, DS, MC, VI. Dressy casual. Ø Cocktails & lounge. Attractive setting with indoor and outdoor seating. Relaxing atmosphere with picturesque views of gondola canals and Las Vegas Strip. **Reservations:** Suggested. **Services:** On-site and valet parking. **Menu:** Modern French cuisine with classic influences. A la carte.

MICHAEL'S ♦♦♦♦ Continental
(702) 737-7111 Dinner $30-70
1¾ mi S on the Strip; in Barbary Coast Hotel, 3595 Las Vegas Bl S.
Open 6-11 pm. Semi-formal attire. Cocktails. Cozy and romantic, attentive service by highly qualified and friendly staff. Located in the heart of the Las Vegas Strip. **Reservations:** Suggested. **Services:** On-site and valet parking. **Menu:** A la carte.

NERO'S STEAK AND SEAFOOD ♦♦♦ Steak & Seafood
(702) 731-7110 Dinner $26-49
I-15 exit E Flamingo, 4½ mi S, on the Strip; inside Caesars Palace, 3570 Las Vegas Bl S.
Open 5:30-10:30 pm, Fri & Sat-11 pm. AE, CB, DC, DS, MC, VI. Dressy casual. Ø Cocktails & lounge. **Reservations:** Suggested. **Services:** On-site and valet parking. **Menu:** A la carte.

OLIVES AT BELLAGIO ♦♦♦ Mediterranean
(702) 693-8181 Lunch $8-20, dinner $12-41
I-15 exit E Flamingo Av, on the Strip; in Bellagio, 3600 Las Vegas Bl S.
Open 11 am-3 & 5-11:30 pm. AE, DC, DS, MC, VI. Casual dress. Cocktails & lounge. Casual Mediterranean cafe with an upbeat atmosphere. Choose from an international list of wines. A great place to meet and relax. **Reservations:** Suggested. **Services:** On-site and valet parking. **Menu:** A la carte.

PASTA PALACE
(702) 432-7777

♦♦ Italian
Dinner $9-24

Boulder Hwy; inside Boulder Station Hotel Casino, 4111 Boulder Hwy.
Open 5 pm-10 pm, Fri-Sat to 11 pm, Sun 3-9 pm. AE, DC, DS, MC, VI. Casual dress. Cocktails. Authentic Italian atmosphere. **Reservations:** Suggested. **Services:** On-site and valet parking. **Menu:** Fresh pasta, pizza and other traditional favorites.

PICASSO
(702) 693-7111

♦♦♦♦♦ French
Dinner $75-85

I-15 exit Flamingo E, on the Strip; in Bellagio, 3600 Las Vegas Bl S.
Open 6-10 pm. Closed Wed. AE, CB, DC, DS, MC, VI. Semi-formal attire. Smoke-free premises. ⊘ Cocktails & lounge. Mediterranean-style restaurant featuring original paintings and ceramics by Pablo Picasso. The flower-filled dining room overlooks the Bellagio fountain. Choose from two tasting dinners created by award-winning chef Julian Serrano. Impeccable service, accomplished staff. **Reservations:** Suggested. **Services:** On-site and valet parking. **Menu:** Prix fixe.

PIERO'S
(702) 369-2305

♦♦♦ Italian
Dinner $19-65

I-15 E 2 mi on Sahara, ½ mi S on Paradise Rd; opposite convention center; 355 Convention Center Dr.
Open 5:30-10 pm. Closed Thanksgiving, 12/24-25. AE, CB, DC, DS, MC, VI. Casual dress. ⊘ Cocktails & lounge; entertainment. **Reservations:** Suggested. **Services:** Valet parking. **Menu:** Osso Buco and fresh seafood dishes.

PHILIPS SUPPER HOUSE
(702) 873-5222

♦♦♦ American
Dinner $9-50

2¾ mi W of the Strip, between Arville St and Decatur Bl; 4545 W Sahara Av.
Open 4-11 pm. AE, CB, DC, DS, MC, VI. **Reservations:** Suggested. Casual dress. ⊘ Cocktails & lounge. **Services:** On-site parking. **Menu:** Prime eastern beef, seafood and Italian specialties. Early-bird specials, carryout.

PRIME STEAKHOUSE
(702) 693-7111

♦♦♦ Steak House
Dinner $20-69

I-15 on the Strip; in Bellagio, 3600 Las Vegas Bl S.
Open 5:30-10:30 pm. AE, CB, DC, DS, MC, VI. Dressy casual. ⊘ Cocktails & lounge. Extensive wine list. Exquisite decor. Located on the waterfront. **Reservations:** Suggested. **Services:** On-site and valet parking. **Menu:** Prime meats, chops and seafood. A la carte.

PRIMO'S - A PLACE FOR STEAKS
(702) 636-7111

♦♦♦ Steak House
Dinner $13-37

I-95 exit Summerlin Pkwy; inside Suncoast Hotel & Casino, 9090 Alta Dr.
Open 5-10 pm. AE, CB, DC, DS, MC, VI. Dressy casual. ⊘ Cocktails & lounge. **Reservations:** Suggested. **Services:** On-site and valet parking. **Menu:** Steaks.

RANGE STEAKHOUSE AT HARRAH'S
(702) 369-5000

♦♦♦ Steak House
Dinner $20-45

I-15 exit E Flamingo; inside Harrah's-Las Vegas, 3475 Las Vegas Bl S.
Open 5:30-10:30 pm, Sat to 11:30 pm. AE, DC, DS, MC, VI. Dressy casual. ⊘ Cocktails & lounge; entertainment. **Reservations:** Suggested. **Services:** On-site and valet parking. **Menu:** A la carte.

RENOIR
♦♦♦♦♦ French

(702) 791-7353
Dinner $30-95

I-15 E Flamingo to Las Vegas Bl; in the Mirage, 3400 Las Vegas Bl S.
Open 6-10:30 pm. Closed Mon. AE, CB, DC, DS, MC, VI. Semi-formal attire. Ø Smoke-free premises. Cocktails. Innovative menu. Elegant dining room. Extensive wine list emphasizing French selections. **Reservations:** Suggested. **Services:** On-site and valet parking. **Menu:** Mediterranean-inspired French cuisine. A la carte and prix fixe pricing.

RISTORANTE ITALIANO
♦♦♦ Italian

(702) 794-9363
Dinner $12-37

I-15 exit E Sahara, on Las Vegas Strip; inside Riviera Hotel and Casino, 2901 Las Vegas Bl S.
Open 5:30-11 pm. Closed Thanksgiving, 12/25; also Wed-Thu 12/1-12/31. AE, CB, DC, DS, MC, VI. Casual dress. Ø Cocktails & lounge; minimum charge $5. **Reservations:** Suggested. **Services:** On-site and valet parking. **Menu:** Italian. A la carte.

SACRED SEA ROOM
♦♦♦ Seafood

(702) 262-4772
Dinner $20-48

I-15 exit E Tropicana, just S on the Strip; in Luxor Las Vegas, 3900 Las Vegas Bl S.
Open 5-11 pm. AE, CB, DC, DS, MC, VI. Dressy casual. Cocktails & lounge. Fish shipped in daily. Friendly service in a dining room furnished in murals and reproductions of fishing on the Nile. **Reservations:** Suggested. **Services:** On-site and valet parking. **Menu:** Fresh- and saltwater fish. A la carte.

SAMBA GRILL
♦♦♦ Brazilian

(702) 791-7337
Dinner $17-30

I-15 exit E Flamingo to Las Vegas Bl; in the Mirage, 3400 Las Vegas Bl S.
Open 5:30-11 pm, Fri-Sat to midnight. AE, CB, DC, DS, MC, VI. Casual dress. Ø Cocktails & lounge. **Reservations:** Suggested. **Services:** On-site and valet parking. **Menu:** Rodizio cooking-style meats, chicken and fish, skewered and carved table side along with traditional Brazilian side dishes.

THE STEAKHOUSE AT CAMELOT
♦♦♦ Steak House

(702) 597-7449
Dinner $10-46

I-15 exit E Tropicana, on the Strip; in Excalibur Hotel & Casino, 3850 Las Vegas Bl S.
Open 5-10 pm, Fri-Sat to 11 pm. AE, CB, DC, DS, MC, VI. Casual dress. Ø Cocktails & lounge. Fine wines and delicious desserts. **Reservations:** Suggested. **Services:** On-site and valet parking. **Menu:** Quality steaks.

STEFANO'S
♦♦♦ Italian

(702) 385-7111
Dinner $14-30

Downtown; casino center area; in Golden Nugget Hotel, 129 E Fremont St.
Open 6-11 pm, Fri-Sat from 5:30 pm. AE, CB, DC, DS, MC, VI. Dressy casual. Ø Cocktails. Very nicely appointed, romantic Italian countryside setting. Hand-blown glass chandeliers and fresh flowers. Friendly and talented singing waiters serve creative, flavorful dishes. **Reservations:** Suggested. **Services:** On-site and valet parking. **Menu:** Italian.

3950 RESTAURANT
♦♦♦♦ Continental

(702) 632-7414
Dinner $27-58

I-15 exit E Tropicana, just S; inside Mandalay Bay Resort & Casino, 3950 Las Vegas Bl S.
Open 5:30-11 pm. AE, CB, DS, MC, VI. Dressy casual. Ø Smoke-free premises.

Cocktails & lounge. **Reservations:** Suggested. **Services:** On-site and valet parking. **Menu:** A la carte.

TILLERMAN ♦♦♦ Steak & Seafood
(702) 731-4036 Dinner $20-49
3½ mi E of Las Vegas Bl S; 2245 E Flamingo Rd.
Open 5-10:30 pm, Fri-Sat to 11 pm. Closed major holidays. AE, CB, DC, DS, MC, VI. Casual dress. ⊘ Cocktails. Unique and comfortable decor. Friendly service in dining room and lounge. **Reservations:** Suggested. **Services:** On-site parking. **Menu:** Fresh seafood and steak.

YOLIE'S BRAZILIAN STEAK HOUSE ♦♦ Ethnic
(702) 794-0700 Lunch $7-15, dinner $13-25
On upper level, Citybank Park Plaza; 3900 Paradise Rd.
Open Mon-Fri 11 am-3 & daily 5-11 pm. AE. Closed 12/25. Dressy casual. ⊘ Cocktails & lounge; entertainment, minimum charge $5. Informal atmosphere. **Reservations:** Suggested. **Services:** On-site parking. **Menu:** Variety of meats served from a skewer, plus lamb, chicken and fish specialties. A la carte, children's menu.

Laughlin

Lodging

AVI HOTEL & CASINO 🅐🅐 ♦♦♦ Hotel
(702) 535-5555 Rates not provided
9 mi S on Needles Hwy via Casino Dr; from I-40, exit W Broadway, 12 mi N; 10000 Aha Macav Pkwy.
AE, DS, MC, VI. Gift shop, casino. 4 stories; interior corridors. **Rooms:** 300. Some shower baths, some whirlpools, ⊘. Roll-in showers. **Recreation:** Pools, whirlpool, exercise room, rental boats, marina, golf, game room. **Services:** Valet parking, laundry, business services. **Dining:** Dining room; coffee shop; deli buffet; $6-20; 24 hrs; cocktails.

COLORADO BELLE HOTEL & CASINO ♦♦ Hotel
(702) 298-4000 Rates not provided
3 mi S of Davis Dam; 2100 S Casino Dr.
AE, CB, DI, DS, MC, VI. Gift shop. 6 stories; interior/exterior corridors. **Rooms:** 1201. Shower bath, some whirlpools, safes, ⊘. Roll-in showers, ▣. **Recreation:** Pools, whirlpool, game room. **Services:** Valet parking, business services.

DON LAUGHLIN'S RIVERSIDE RESORT HOTEL & CASINO ♦♦♦ Hotel
(702) 298-2535 Rates not provided
2 mi S of Davis Dam; 1650 S Casino Dr.
AE, DI, DS, MC, VI. Small pets only, $8 extra charge; $100 deposit. Gift shop. **Rooms:** 1404. Some shower baths, some whirlpools, ⊘. Roll-in showers, ▣. **Recreation:** Pools, whirlpool, massage, game room. **Services:** Valet parking, business services.

EDGEWATER HOTEL/CASINO 🅐🅐 ♦♦♦ Hotel
(702) 298-2453 $22-300
2⅛ mi S of Davis Dam; 2020 S Casino Dr.

XP $4. 3-day refund notice; cancellation fee. AE, CB, DI, DS, MC, VI. Gift shop. 3-26 stories; interior corridors. **Rooms:** 1419. Some shower baths, some whirlpools. Roll-in showers, ▦. **Recreation:** Pools, whirlpool, game room, ⊘. **Services:** Valet parking, laundry, business services. **Dining:** Dining room; 2 restaurants; coffee shop; deli; buffet; $5-25; 24 hrs; cocktails.

FLAMINGO LAUGHLIN   Not Rated
(702) 298-5111   Rates not provided
2 mi S of Davis Dam; 1900 S Casino Dr.
Management refused evaluation. Facilities, services, and decor characterize a midrange property. ⊘ 🔲 ▦

GOLDEN NUGGET LAUGHLIN   ♦♦♦ Hotel
(702) 298-7111   Rates not provided
3½ mi S of Davis Dam; 2300 S Casino Dr.
AE, DS, MC, VI. Gift shop. 4 stories; interior corridors. **Rooms:** 300. Some shower baths, ⊘. Roll-in showers, ▦. **Recreation:** Pools, whirlpool, game room. **Services:** Valet parking, laundry.

HARRAH'S CASINO HOTEL   ♦♦♦ Hotel
(702) 298-4600   Rates not provided
5 mi S of Davis Dam, on the river; 2900 S Casino Dr.
AE, CB, DI, DS, MC, VI. Gift shop. 20 stories; exterior corridors. **Rooms:** 1600. Some shower baths, ⊘. Roll-in showers. **Recreation:** Pools, whirlpools, massage, game room. **Services:** Valet parking, laundry, business services. **Dining:** See listing for William Fisk's Steakhouse.

RAMADA EXPRESS HOTEL & CASINO   ♦♦♦ Hotel
(702) 298-4200 $19-95
3 mi S of Davis Dam; 2121 S Casino Dr.
XP $7. AE, CB, DI, DS, MC, VI. Gift shop. 12-24 stories; interior corridors. **Rooms:** 1501. Some shower baths, some whirlpools, ⊘. Roll-in showers, ▦. **Recreation:** Pools, whirlpool. **Services:** Valet parking, laundry, business services.

Restaurants

THE GOURMET ROOM   ♦♦♦ Continental
(702) 298-2535   Dinner $19-35
In Don Laughlin's Riverside Resort Hotel & Casino, 1650 Casino Dr.
Open 5-10 pm, Sat to 11 pm. AE, CB, DC, DS, MC, VI. Relaxing atmosphere with great river views. Casual dress. ⊘ Cocktails & lounge. **Reservations:** Suggested. **Services:** On-site and valet parking. **Menu:** Continental.

MISSISSIPPI LOUNGE AND SEAFOOD BAR   ♦♦ Seafood
(702) 298-4000   Lunch & dinner $6-10
In Colorado Belle Hotel & Casino, 2100 S Casino Dr.
Open noon-10 pm, Sat to 11 pm. AE, CB, DC, DS, MC, VI. Located upstairs in Colorado Belle Hotel & Casino, overlooking the Colorado River. Casual and friendly atmosphere. Casual dress. Cocktails & lounge. **Services:** On-site and valet parking. **Menu:** Seafood specialties include peel-and-eat shrimp.

WILLIAM FISK'S STEAKHOUSE ♦♦♦ American

(702) 298-4600 Dinner $18-45

In Harrah's Casino Hotel, 2900 S Casino Dr.

Open 5-10 pm, Fri-Sat 11 to pm. AE, DC, DS, MC, VI. Intimate dining atmosphere, overlooking Colorado River. Casual dress. ∅ Cocktails. **Reservations:** Suggested. **Services:** On-site and valet parking. **Menu:** A la carte.

Primm

Lodging

BUFFALO BILL'S RESORT & CASINO ♦♦ Hotel

(702) 382-1212 Rates not provided

45 mi S of Las Vegas via I-15, exit State Line; just E.

AE, CB, DI, DS, MC, VI. Gift shop. 16 stories; interior corridors. **Rooms:** 1240. Some whirlpools. Roll-in showers, ☒. **Recreation:** Pools, whirlpool, seasonal pool, golf, putting green. **Services:** Valet parking, laundry, business services.

PRIMM VALLEY RESORT & CASINO ♦♦♦ Motor Inn

(702) 382-1212 Rates not provided

45 mi S of Las Vegas via I-15, exit State Line.

AE, DI, DS, MC, VI. Gift shop. 4 stories; interior corridors. **Rooms:** 623. Some shower baths, some whirlpools, ∅. ⬛, roll-in showers, ☒. **Recreation:** Pools, whirlpool, putting green, playground, golf, game room. **Services:** Valet parking, laundry, business services. **Dining:** See listing for GP's Restaurant.

WHISKEY PETE'S HOTEL & CASINO ♦♦ Hotel

(702) 382-1212 Rates not provided

45 mi S of Las Vegas, W of and adj to I-15; exit State Line.

AE, DI, DS, MC, VI. Gift shop. 2-19 stories; interior corridors. **Rooms:** 777. Some shower baths, some whirlpools, ∅. Roll-in showers, ☒. **Recreation:** Pools, whirlpool, waterslide, golf. **Services:** Valet parking, laundry, business services.

Restaurant

GP'S RESTAURANT ♦♦♦ American

(702) 382-1212 Dinner $13-15

45 mi S of Las Vegas via I-15, exit State Line; in Primm Valley Resort & Casino.

Open Wed-Sun 5-10 pm, Sat to 11 pm. Closed Mon-Tue. AE, CB, DC, MC, VI. Attractive with comfortable booth and table seating. ∅ Cocktails. **Reservations:** Suggested. **Services:** On-site and valet parking. **Menu:** Specializes in prime rib and seafood, including lobster. A la carte.

Bullhead City, Arizona

Lodging

BEST WESTERN BULLHEAD CITY INN ⒶⒶ
♦♦♦ Motel
(928) 754-3000 — Rates not provided
1¾ mi S of Laughlin Bridge, then just E on 3rd St; 1126 Hwy 95.
AE, CB, DI, DS, MC, VI. Pets, $5 extra charge; $25 deposit. 2 stories; exterior corridors.
Rooms: 88. Safes, ⊘. ⌧ **Recreation:** Whirlpool. **Services:** Laundry, business services.

DAYS INN
♦ Motel
(928) 758-1711
3⁹⁄₁₀ mi S of Laughlin Bridge on SR 95, then just E; 2200 Rancho Colorado.
AE, DI, DS, MC, VI. Small pets only, $20 extra charge. 3 stories; interior corridors.
Rooms: 70. Some shower baths, ⊘. Roll-in showers, ⌧. **Recreation:** Whirlpool.
Services: Laundry.

LAKE MOHAVE RESORT ⒶⒶ
♦ Resort
(928) 754-3245 — Rates not provided
3 mi N of Davis Dam, in Lake Mead NRA.
DS, MC, VI. Pets, $5 extra charge. 2 stories; exterior corridors. **Rooms:** 51. Some
shower baths. **Recreation:** Rental boats, marina, water-skiing, fishing. **Dining:**
Restaurant; 8 am-8 pm, Fri-Sat to 9 pm; $9-16; cocktails.

LODGE ON THE RIVER ⒶⒶ
♦♦ Motel
(928) 758-8080 — Rates not provided
3¾ mi S of Laughlin Bridge; 1717 Hwy 95.
AE, CB, DI, DS, MC, VI. Pets; $20 deposit. 2 stories; exterior corridors. **Rooms:** 64.
Some shower baths, ⊘. Roll-in showers. **Services:** Laundry.

SHANGRI-LA LODGE
♦♦ Extended Stay Motel
(928) 758-1117 — Rates not provided
2 mi S of Laughlin Bridge; 1767 Georgia Ln.
DS, MC, VI. Small pets only. 2 stories; exterior corridors. **Rooms:** 28. ⊘ **Services:**
Laundry.

SUNRIDGE HOTEL & CONFERENCE CENTER ⒶⒶ
♦♦♦ Motor Inn
(928) 754-4700 — Rates not provided
3½ mi N of town on SR 68, then just S; 839 Landon Dr.
Continental breakfast. AE, CB, DI, DS, MC, VI. Small pets only; $100 deposit. 4 sto-
ries; exterior corridors. **Rooms:** 148. ⊘ ⌧ **Recreation:** Whirlpool, exercise room.
Services: Laundry, business services.

Restaurant

TOWNE'S SQUARE CAFE
♦♦ American
(520) 763-2477 — Lunch $5-7, dinner $7-12
3⁹⁄₁₀ mi S of Laughlin Bridge; 1751 W Hwy 95, Ste 25.
Open 6 am-10 pm. Closed 12/25. AE, DC, DS, MC, VI. Casual dress. ⊘ Beer & wine
only. Nice family-style restaurant with homey decor and atmosphere. **Services:** On-site
parking. **Menu:** Good selection of sandwiches, beef, chicken and seafood entrees.
Children's menu, carryout.

Campgrounds & Trailer Parks

*Warm weather, and nearby scenic and recreation areas attract thousands of campers to Las Vegas and Laughlin every year. Camping accommodations range from simple RV lots located close to the gambling action and glitz to more rugged settings in surrounding areas, including Bullhead City, Arizona. The campgrounds in this section are listed alphabetically by city or closest recreation area—**Boulder City, Lake Mead National Recreation Area** (Lake Mead and Lake Mohave), **Las Vegas, Primm, Red Rock Canyon National Conservation Area, Spring Mountains National Recreation Area, Valley of Fire State Park** and **Bullhead City, Arizona**. Unless otherwise noted, campgrounds are open all year.*

The following listings show the nightly camping fee for the number of people specified, including a recreational vehicle or automobile (with or without a trailer). Electricity, water and sewer RV hookups are indicated by the letters E, W and S, respectively.

Private campgrounds have been inspected by an Auto Club representative and meet AAA requirements for recommendation. Private campgrounds that did not meet the requirements for listing or that were not inspected have not been included in this book.

Public campgrounds typically allow a more natural experience or have fewer services, and as a result usually do not meet AAA requirements for recommendation; they are listed here as a service. Information for the public campgrounds was obtained from the administering government agency, which is shown at the end of the individual listings, i.e., National Forest (NF); National Park Service (NPS); Bureau of Land Management (BLM); State; County; and Private.

The 🅐🅐🅐 in a private campground listing identifies the establishment as a AAA Official Appointment; it indi-

cates that the campground has expressed a particular interest in serving AAA members. In order to communicate this desire to the traveling public, these facilities have purchased the right to display the AAA emblem.

Bringing the family pet? Pets on leashes are welcome in most campgrounds. Leashes should be no longer than 6 feet. Be aware that some campgrounds charge a nominal fee for pets (these are noted).

For an additional fee, an RV towing and tire-change service option is available for motorhomes, campers and travel/camping trailers. Call (800) AAA-HELP; hearing impaired call (800) 955-4TDD.

Reservations

Most private campgrounds listed here accept reservations by phone. Those public campgrounds that are reservable include the appropriate contact information in the section head or individual campground listing. Otherwise, camping is "first come, first served."

Additional fees may be charged for some services and facilities, such as showers, laundry, and recreational activities or equipment. Swimming pools may or may not be heated.

Where accepted, major credit cards honored by the campgrounds appear in each listing and are abbreviated as follows: AE=American Express, CB=Carte Blanche, DI=Diners Club, DS=Discover, MC=MasterCard, VI=VISA.

All camping fees are subject to change.

Boulder City

BOULDER OAKS RV RESORT
(702) 294-4425
1010 Industrial Rd.

Private
$23-30 for 4

DS, MC, VI. Pets. Some sites with view of distant Lake Mead. El 2507. 24 acres. **Sites:** 275 RV sites; length restrictions; EWS; 50 amps; phone and cable TV hookups. **Facilities:** Flush toilets. **Recreation:** Pool, sauna, whirlpool, recreation rm. **Services:** Laundry.

Lake Mead National Recreation Area

HEADQUARTERS
(702) 293-8990, 293-8907
25 mi SE of Las Vegas; 601 Nevada Hwy, Boulder City.
Unless noted otherwise, the maximum stay for camping in the Lake Mead National Recreation Area is 30 consecutive days, with a cumulative total of 90 camping days in a consecutive 12-month period. All public campgrounds at lakes Mead and Mohave are first come, first served.

Lake Mead

BOULDER BEACH
6 mi NE of Boulder City on SR 166.

NPS
$10 for 8

Pets. **Sites:** 140 tent/RV sites. **Facilities:** Disposal station; flush toilets; grills; picnic tables. **Recreation:** Boats, boat ramp. **Services:** Groceries, laundry.

CALLVILLE BAY
22 mi NE of Henderson on SR 147/167.

NPS
$10 for 8

Pets. **Sites:** 157 tent/RV sites. **Facilities:** Disposal station; piped water; flush toilets; showers; grills; picnic tables. **Recreation:** Boats, boat ramp. **Services:** Laundry.

ECHO BAY
30 mi S of Overton on SR 167.

NPS
$10 for 8

Pets. **Sites:** 155 tent/RV sites. **Facilities:** Disposal station; water; flush toilets; showers; grills; picnic tables. **Recreation:** Boats, boat ramp. **Services:** Laundry.

LAS VEGAS BAY
8 mi NE of Henderson or 13 mi NW of Boulder City on SR 166.

NPS
$10 for 8

Pets. **Sites:** 86 tent/RV sites. **Facilities:** Disposal station; flush toilets; showers; grills; picnic tables. **Recreation:** Boats, boat ramp.

TEMPLE BAR
26 mi E of Boulder City on US 93, then 28 mi N on Temple Bar access rd.

NPS
$10 for 8

Pets. **Sites:** 166 tent/RV sites. **Facilities:** Disposal station; water; flush toilets; showers;

grills; picnic tables. **Recreation:** Marina, boats, boat ramp, boat and auto fuel. **Services:** Laundry, groceries.

Lake Mohave

COTTONWOOD COVE
NPS
14 mi E of Searchlight on US 95.
$10 for 8
15-night max stay in lower campground. Pets. **Sites:** 145 tent/RV sites. **Facilities:** Disposal station; flush toilets; grills; picnic tables. **Recreation:** Boats, boat ramp. **Services:** Laundry, groceries.

COTTONWOOD COVE RESORT & MARINA ⒶⒶⒶ
Private
(702) 297-1464
$17-$21.45 for 8
Between Las Vegas and Needles; 14 mi E of Searchlight, off US 95 at Lake Mohave.
10 am check out. AE, DS, MC, VI. Pets. Desert landscape. **Sites:** 73 RV; EWS. **Facilities:** Disposal station; piped water; flush toilets; showers; air conditioning ($3). **Recreation:** Beach, swimming, fishing, boat ramp, marina, houseboats, powerboats, personal watercraft, water-skiing and equipment. **Services:** Laundry, groceries, propane. **Dining:** Cafe.

KATHERINE LANDING
NPS
(702) 293-8907, (928) 754-3272
$10 for 8
6 mi N of Bullhead City, off US 95/SR 68.
Sites: 172 tent/RV sites. **Facilities:** Disposal station; water; flush toilets; showers; grills; picnic tables. **Recreation:** Boats, boat ramp, fishing, swimming. **Services:** Laundry.

Katherine Landing, on Lake Mohave, has full marina services in addition to camping facilities.

Las Vegas

ARIZONA CHARLIE'S EAST RV PARK
Private
(702) 951-5911
$18 for 2
4445 Boulder Hwy.
Deposit required; handling fee. Weekly rates available. AE, DS, MC, VI. Small pets only, $2 extra charge. 11 acres. **Sites:** 239 RV sites; EWS; 50 amps. **Facilities:** Flush toilets, phone hookups. **Recreation:** Pool, whirlpool, exercise room, putting green, recreation room, pool table. **Services:** Propane, area transportation, laundry.

BOULDER LAKES RV RESORT
Private
(702) 435-1157
$22 for 4
1 mi E of I-515/SR 93 and 95, exit Russell Rd, ⅓ mi N at Desert Horizons Rd. 6201 Boulder Hwy.
XP $3. Deposit required; handling fee. Weekly and monthly rates available. MC, VI. Small pets only. Desert atmosphere, paved roads and pads. 10 acres. **Sites:** 417 level RV sites, no pull-thrus; 50' RV limit; EWS; 50 amps. **Facilities:** Flush toilets; phone and cable TV hookups. **Recreation:** Pool, saunas, whirlpools. **Services:** Groceries, laundry.

CIRCUSLAND RV PARK
Private
(702) 734-0410
$13-24 for 8
I-15, exit Sahara Blvd, ¾ mi E; adj to Circus Circus Hotel, Casino & Theme Park. 500 Circus Circus Dr (Enter off Industrial Rd).
14-night max stay. Deposit required. Senior discount. AE, CB, DC, DS, MC, VI. Pets. 35 acres. **Sites:** 399 paved RV sites, many pull-thrus; 378 EW, 365 S; 50 amps. **Facilities:** Dump station; flush toilets. **Recreation:** Pool, whirlpool, playground. **Services:** Groceries, laundry.

DESTINY OASIS LAS VEGAS RV RESORT
Private
(702) 260-2020
$20-57
Exit I-15 at Blue Diamond Rd (exit 33), 1½ mi E to Las Vegas Bl , ½ mi S; 2711 W Windmill.
AE, DS, MC, VI. Small pets only. 46 acres. **Sites:** 702 RV sites, mostly pull-thrus; EWS; 50 amps. **Facilities:** Dump station; flush toilets; phone and cable TV hookups. **Recreation:** Pool, whirlpool, recreation room, exercise room, 18-hole putting course on natural turf greens. **Services:** Groceries, propane, laundry. **Dining:** Lounge.

LAS VEGAS KOA RESORT
Private
(702) 451-5527
$24.95-32.95 for 2
4 mi SE on US 93 and 95, just S of Desert Inn Rd; 4315 Boulder Hwy.
XP $3-5. Deposit required. Monthly rates available. DS, MC, VI. Pets. 20 acres. **Sites:** 300 (60 tent, 240 RV) most pull-thru sites level and shaded, with gravel pads; 240 EW, 180 S; 50 amps. **Recreation:** Pool, whirlpool, wading pool 5/15-9/15, sports court, recreation room, miniature golf, playground. **Facilities:** Dump station; flush toilets; phone hookups. **Services:** Groceries, propane, area and Strip transportation, laundry, self service RV and car wash.

RV camping facilities in Las Vegas generally feature swimming pools, recreation rooms and convenient access to casino entertainment.

Laughlin

AVI RV PARK   Private
(702) 535-5555 $17-27 for 4
9 mi s on Needles Hwy via Casino Dr; from I-40, exit W Broadway, 12 mi N. 10000 Aha Macav Pkwy.
Deposit required; handling fee. Weekly and monthly rates available. AE, DS, MC, VI. Pets. On the Colorado River, adjacent to casino. No shade. 25 acres. **Sites:** 257 RV sites, gravel, level and some pull-thrus; EWS; 50 amps, $3 extra charge; cable TV hookups. **Facilities:** Flush toilets, lounge. **Recreation:** Beach, pool, whirlpool, swimming, boat ramp, marina, rental boats. **Services:** Laundry.

Primm

PRIMADONNA RV VILLAGE   Private
(702) 679-5744 $10-50
I-15, exit Stateline, just E, 45 mi S of Las Vegas.
Deposit required. 56-night max stay. AE, DC, DS, MC, VI. Pets; dogs & cats only. El 2700. 40 acres. **Sites:** 197 RV sites, mostly pull-thru; EWS; 50 amps. **Facilities:** Dump station, flush toilets, barbecues. **Recreation:** Pool, whirlpool, golf, playground. **Services:** Groceries, propane, area and casino transportation, laundry.

Red Rock Canyon National Conservation Area

LAS VEGAS FIELD OFFICE
(702) 647-5000
4765 W Vegas Dr, Las Vegas.

Red Rock Canyon Visitor Center
(702) 363-1921
1000 Scenic Dr, Las Vegas.

13-Mile Campground   BLM
At the 13-mile market on SR 159/W Charleston Bl. $10
Maximum 14-consecutive-night stay in any 30-day period. First come, first served. Pets, $3. El 3100. **Sites:** 66 sites (14 tent, 52 tent/RV). **Facilities:** Primitive toilets; barbecue pits; picnic tables. **Services:** Visitor center 2 mi W of campground.

Spring Mountains National Recreation Area

HEADQUARTERS
(702) 873-8800

Humboldt-Toiyabe National Forest
1200 Franklin Way, Sparks, NV.

Spring Mountains National Recreation Area
2881 S Valley View, Ste 16, Las Vegas.

35 mi NW of Las Vegas via US 95, turnoff at SR 157/Kyle Canyon Rd or SR 156/Lee Canyon Rd. Within Humboldt-Toiyabe National Forest. Campgrounds open daily May through mid-Oct; early and late season may vary due to the weather. Maximum 14-consecutive-night stay in any 30-day period.

For campsite reservations up to 240 days in advance, contact the National Recreation Reservation Service toll free at (877) 444-6777, (877) 833-6777 (TDD), or access their website at reserveusa.com. Reservation hours are 10 am to 7 pm EST. $9 non-refundable reservation fee; 3-night refund notice; $10 service fee for cancellations or changes; $20 no-show fee. AE, DS, MC and VI are accepted.

Unless indicated, the maximum RV length is 30 ft.

Dolomite   NF
43 mi from Las Vegas in Lee Canyon on SR 156. $13 per family
$5 per additional vehicle. Pets. El 8400. **Sites:** 31 tent/RV. **Facilities:** Piped water; flush and primitive toilets; no showers; barbecues; fire rings; picnic tables. **Recreation:** Nature trails.

Fletcher View   NF
34½ mi from Las Vegas in Kyle Canyon on SR 157.   13 per family
$5 per additional vehicle. First come, first served. El 7200. Sites: 12 tent/RV; 25-ft maximum RV length. **Facilities:** Piped water; primitive toilets; no showers; barbecues, fire rings; some picnic tables. Recreation: Riding stable within 1 mile.

Hilltop NF
15 mi NW on US 95, 17 mi W on SR 157, 6 mi NW on SR 158. (Due to short parking spurs and a narrow approach road, this campground is not recommended for trailers and motorhomes.)
$13 per family
$5 per additional vehicle. PNRS. El 8400. **Sites:** 31 tent/RV; 2 sites wheelchair accessible. **Facilities:** Piped water; flush toilets; showers; barbecues, fire rings; picnic tables. **Recreation:** Nature trails.

Kyle Canyon NF
15 mi NW on US 95, 17½ mi W on SR 157. $13 per family
$5 per additional vehicle. PNRS. El 7000. **Sites:** 19 tent/RV sites; 9 sites wheelchair accessible. **Facilities:** Piped water; primitive toilets; no showers; barbecues, fire rings; picnic tables. **Recreation:** Riding stable within 1 mile.

McWilliams NF
In Lee Canyon, 43 mi from Las Vegas in Lee Canyon on SR 156. $13 per family
$5 per additional vehicle. PNRS. El 8400. **Sites:** 31 tent/RV; 2 sites wheelchair accessible. **Facilities:** Piped water; flush and primitive toilets; no showers; barbecues, fire rings; picnic tables. **Recreation:** Horseshoe pit.

Valley of Fire State Park

VALLEY OF FIRE STATE PARK VISITOR CENTER
(702) 397-2088
50 mi NE of Las Vegas via I-15 and SR 169.

Valley of Fire Campgrounds State
2 mi W of the visitor center. $13 per vehicle
First-come, first-served. Pets. **Sites:** 51 sites (48 tent/RV, 3 tent); 2 wheelchair-accessible sites. **Facilities:** Piped water; flush and primitive toilets; showers; barbecues, fire rings; picnic tables. **Recreation:** Nature trails.

Bullhead City, Arizona

DAVIS CAMP COUNTY PARK County
(928) 754-7250 $10-16
1 mi N on SR 95; below Davis Dam.
14-night max stay, on beach. MC, VI. Pets. Hospital in town. 365 acres, on Colorado River. **Sites:** 140 RV sites; 110 EWS, 30 EW; unlimited beach camping; 50' RV limit. **Facilities:** Dump station; flush toilets. **Recreation:** Boating, fishing, swimming, boat ramp, dock. **Services:** Laundry, 24-hr attendant, visitor center.

SNOWBIRD RV RESORT Private
(928) 768-7141 $16 for 2
13¾ mi S of Laughlin Bridge on SR 95, then just E; 1600 Joy Ln.
XP $3. Pets $11 extra charge. 5 acres. **Sites:** 135 (10 tent, 125 RV); 135 EW, 125 S; 50 amps($3 6/1-8/31); air conditioning ($3); washer/dryer hookup ($1). **Facilities:** Flush toilets. **Recreation:** Pool, whirlpool golf, recreation room. **Services:** Laundry.

Index

This index contains listings for points of interest, recreational activities, events and services.

Acknowledgements

Writer	Jordan R. Young
Cartographer	Anna Davila
Graphic Artist	Stephen O. Schilling
Editor	Kristine Miller

Photography

Todd Masinter............................6, 37, 39, 48, 67, 68, 72 (both)

David J. Brackney...10, 83, 97

Robert Brown....................................5, 23, 64, 75 (both), 86, 87

Chris Hart 11, 102, 148

Jordan R. Young.............9, 13, 19, 27, 40, 42, 43, 45, 47, 54, 70

Boulder City Museum & Historical Association 61

Circus Circus Hotel & Casino 151

Flamingo Las Vegas 53

Las Vegas News Bureau.....15, 38, 55, 57, 59, 73 (both), 82, 93, 99

Liberace Museum ....39 (bottom)

McCarran International Airport 107

Scandia Family Fun Center...44

Scenic Air...51

University of Nevada, Las Vegas 17

The Venetian 21

Notes

Notes